MEMORIES *of* OLD SUNRISE

Gold Mining on Alaska's Turnagain Arm

Autobiography of
Albert Weldon Morgan

Edited with an Introduction by
Rolfe G. Buzzell

This second edition is published through a three-way partnership among

COOK INLET HISTORICAL SOCIETY

HOPE AND SUNRISE HISTORICAL SOCIETY

KENAI MOUNTAINS-TURNAGAIN ARM NATIONAL HERITAGE AREA
CORRIDOR COMMUNITIES ASSOCIATION

COOK INLET
HISTORICAL SOCIETY

The Cook Inlet Historical Society was incorporated in 1955. The Society's goals include the discovery, preservation, and dissemination of the history of Alaska in general and of the Cook Inlet area in particular. As a support group for the Anchorage Museum at Rasmuson Center, the Society holds regular meetings at the museum. www.cookinlethistory.org

The Hope and Sunrise Historical Society was founded in 1971. The Hope and Sunrise Historical and Mining Museum opened in 1994. The mission of the Hope and Sunrise Historical Society is to preserve the history of the Alaska Gold Rush communities of Hope and Sunrise and to share this history with the public. www.hopeandsunrisehistoricalsociety.org

Kenai Mountains-Turnagain Arm
National Heritage Area

The Kenai Mountains-Turnagain Arm (KMTA) National Heritage Area is one of forty-nine Heritage Areas across the nation and Alaska's first. The KMTA Corridor Communities Association was incorporated in 2000. The KMTA National Heritage Area was established in 2009 through an act of Congress to recognize, preserve, and interpret the historic resources and cultural landscapes of the Kenai Mountains-Turnagain Arm transportation corridor. www.kmtacorridor.org

In this second edition, the photograph credits throughout the text have been updated to reflect changes in name for several libraries and museums in Anchorage, Juneau, and Seward, Alaska.

Copyright © 1994, 2013 by Cook Inlet Historical Society, Anchorage Museum at Rasmuson Center, 625 C Street, Anchorage, AK 99501-3544 USA

Library of Congress
Morgan, Albert Weldon
Memories of Old Sunrise
Gold Mining on Alaska's Turnagain Arm 1897-1901/by Albert Weldon Morgan
Introduction by Rolfe G. Buzzell

Includes index
ISBN 978-1-4675-7760-1
1. Alaska–Description and travel–1897-1901. 2. United States–Mining
International Standard Book Number: 1-878462-01-6
Library of Congress Catalogue Number: 94-68464

Printed in the United States of America.
Second printing book re-design by NANETTE STEVENSON.

TABLE OF CONTENTS

PHOTOGRAPHS AND MAPS

A. W. "Jack" Morgan, late 1950s.

*M*emories of Old Sunrise was written by my grandfather, A. W. "Jack" Morgan, at the grand age of ninety-two. It is his account of his years in Alaska from 1897 to 1901 mining for gold on the Kenai Peninsula. I hope that his recollections will prove to be of value to serious Alaska historians and that they will also provide enjoyment to those who, like myself, have developed a keen interest in the early days of gold mining in Alaska.

My grandfather was born and raised on a small farm near Franklin, North Carolina. About all I know of his parents was that his father had a "Minie ball" left inside his elbow as a result of serving in the Confederacy during the Civil War. At the age of sixteen my grandfather set out on his own as there was not much opportunity for him on the farm or in that part of the country. He worked his way across the country on the railroads to the Pacific Northwest where he found steady work in the logging camps. He was twenty-nine years old and working with a partner as a gippo logger[1] when he decided to try his hand at gold mining in Alaska.

A few years after he returned from Alaska my grandfather and grandmother took a homestead on the Siletz River which is in Lincoln County, Oregon and flows into the Pacific Ocean. He continued to work in logging and over time became recognized as the leading timber cruiser[2] in Lincoln County. In the 1920s or early 1930s he moved to Portland, Oregon, and worked as both a timber cruiser and timber broker. At the age of eighty-eight, he set down his experiences in Lincoln County in his earlier book titled *Fifty Years in Siletz Timber* (published privately in 1959).

I have often marveled at the fact that my grandfather waited until so late in his life to put into writing his many interesting experiences and recollections. I think the answer, in part, lies in the unusual ruggedness of his constitution—both

---

1   A small scale, independent logging contractor.
2   A person who walks timber tracts to determine the type, volume, and value of uncut timber for prospective buyers.

physical and mental. Almost anyone who had walked with him in the woods was ready to attest to his endurance and he remained physically active well into his eighties. He neither drank nor smoked and did not approve of those who did. He never learned to drive an automobile-relying instead on his own two legs or his two sons and five grandsons for his transportation needs. He was a man who did not know the meaning of self-doubt, was set in his ways, had strong opinions on most subjects, was known for his fairness and honesty, and didn't like Democrats in office. He was simply such a strong and vigorous person that I think it was not until his late eighties that he began to realize that he would not be around forever and therefore should commit his recollections to writing.

My grandfather loved the Siletz River country. Some of my earliest memories of him were when he took me fishing in a rowboat on the Siletz for sea-run cutthroat and jack salmon. A few years after he died, my father sold some property on the Siletz to the county with the stipulation that it be used for a park in his memory. Today, picnickers and drift boaters are both able to make use of the "A. W. Morgan County Park" located about fifteen miles up the Siletz just above tidewater.

I have the fondest of memories of my grandfather and *Memories of Old Sunrise* has helped me to know and appreciate him all the more. I hope that all who read it will find it enjoyable and will, like me, be able to derive from it something that is personally meaningful.

Camas, Washington
May 5, 1988

ACKNOWLEDGEMENTS

I would like to acknowledge the libraries, museums, government agencies, private businesses, and individuals who provided assistance in the completion of this project.

Institutions that granted permission to reproduce photographs from their collections for this volume include the Elmer E. Rasmuson Library of the University of Alaska Fairbanks; the Alaska Historical Library in Juneau; the Anchorage Museum of History and Art; the Girdwood Historical Society; the Hope and Sunrise Historical Society in Hope; the Seward Public Library; the United States Geological Survey, Denver, Colorado; the Chugach National Forest, Anchorage; and the publishers of *Alaska Sportsman* in Anchorage.

Special thanks to Donald W. Clickner of Troy, New York, and Gerald C. Lansing of New Brunswick, New York, for allowing reproduction of photographs from their grandfathers' expedition to Turnagain Arm in 1898. Nori Bowman of Fairbanks drew the initial maps. Daniel G. Williams of Aberdeen, Washington, provided explanations of hand logging terms. Steven C. Levi and Mike Burwell of Anchorage helped identify full names of several individuals mentioned in the manuscript. Eva Trautmann, of the publications committee of the Cook Inlet Historical Society, generously shared her time and editorial talents.

A number of members of the Morgan family were also helpful. David Duvall of Franklin, North Carolina, contributed photographs of Jack and Lovicia Morgan in their early years. I am especially grateful to Jack Morgan's three grandsons: Robert J. Morgan of Rainier, Oregon; John Signor of Battleground, Washington; and the late James W. Signor of Portland, Oregon. They provided photographs of Jack and Lovicia Morgan and generously shared their knowledge about their grandparents.

Funding for this project has been provided in part by the State of Alaska, Gold Rush Centennial Task Force.

Rolfe Buzzell
Anchorage, Alaska
June 1994

INTRODUCTION 1994

By Rolfe G. Buzzell, Ph. D.

When Albert Weldon Morgan arrived in south-central Alaska in the spring of 1897, gold mining in the Turnagain Arm area had been underway for several years. Traces of gold were first reported in Alaska by Russians on the Kenai River in 1834 and again in 1850-1851. After the United States purchased Alaska in 1867, American prospectors began to search for precious metals in the largely unmapped territory. Gold was discovered in commercial quantities on tributaries of the upper Yukon River and in southeast Alaska in the 1880s. This led to prospecting in other parts of the territory. In 1890, a prospector named Alexander King paid off his grubstake at the old Russian trading post at Kenai with four pokes of gold obtained from panning on the northern coast of the Kenai Peninsula. Up to that time, the shallow waters and treacherous bore tides of Turnagain Arm had served to keep prospectors away. The discovery of gold by King attracted the attention of local prospectors, and in 1893 and 1894 claims were filed on Resurrection Creek and its tributaries. Discoveries on Canyon and Mills creeks the following year set off the first "rush" in which some 3,000 gold seekers flocked to the Turnagain Arm during 1896.

The large number of miners, the meager amounts of gold found on many of the creeks, and news of a richer gold strike in the Klondike fields of Canada resulted in a sharp drop in the number of people attracted to the Turnagain Arm district in 1897. Like others who arrived in 1897, Morgan found the most promising ground already staked by those who had arrived earlier. Opportunities were scarce for latecomers, who usually had no mining experience and limited money and supplies on which to live. Most were forced to work for wages, hoping to make a grubstake that would enable them to strike out on their own or to buy into a partnership on a good claim. Many exhausted their resources prospecting the less promising creeks or buying claims that proved to be worthless. For most, the dream of striking it rich faded quickly. A second "rush" of 7,000-10,000 people to Cook Inlet occurred in 1898, but it too was short-lived. Thereafter, the number of gold seekers rapidly declined as the disappointed returned to the states or moved on to the more promising prospects in the Klondike and Nome areas. Even Alexander King moved on to the Klondike, where he died on the gallows for killing a partner.

For those who stayed on, the creek gravels—or "placers" as they were called—yielded no better than wages in most cases. Profitable mining was confined to a small number of creeks. Turnagain Arm became a largely forgotten backwater compared to more promising discoveries made elsewhere in Alaska. At the same time, the nature of mining in the Turnagain Arm area was changing. Those who came into the country before 1898 used hand mining methods to work the gravel streams. This usually consisted of shoveling gold bearing gravel into sluice boxes. Water from creeks was diverted through the sluice boxes to wash off the gravel. The heavier gold nuggets and flakes were trapped between riffles—bars or slats set across the bottom of the sluice boxes. As the richer claims were worked out, even greater volumes of gravel had to be shoveled and washed in order to make wages.

Experienced miners from the California gold fields, such as Simon Wible of Bakersfield, arrived in 1898 and 1899 with large amounts of capital to purchase and consolidate claims, hire large crews, dig ditches and build flume systems, and bring in large volumes of metal pipe to undertake hydraulic mining. This method of mining employed large volumes of water under pressure to blast away the gravel hillsides and push the gold bearing gravel through long lines of sluice boxes. By 1901, about the only mining operations making a profit on the "Arm," as the Turnagain Arm area was frequently called, were those engaged in hydraulic technology. At the same time, prospectors were beginning to locate promising hard rock prospects—known as "lodes"—where the gold deposits were still located in place in the native rock.

The limited gold deposits in the creeks of the Turnagain Arm area dictated that future placer mining there would be limited to hydraulicking. The transition from hand mining to hydraulic mining on the Turnagain Arm occurred during the years that A. W. Morgan mined in the district. After Morgan sold the "J. R. No. 2," or the "old Powers claim" as it was called, on Lynx Creek in 1901, he spent the rest of the season working for a hydraulic operator on Canyon Creek. In September, he sold and abandoned his remaining claims and left Alaska for good. He was probably more fortunate than most of his contemporaries, due in large part to his previous mining experience, his business acumen, and his ability to work with and lead people.

The short-lived gold rush to Turnagain Arm had a long term impact on the Cook Inlet area. Prospectors fanned out into the surrounding country, finding

Miners preparing to depart Sunrise for their claims, 1896.
PHOTOGRAPH COURTESY OF U.S. FOREST SERVICE, ANCHORAGE.

new placer deposits in the nearby Yentna and Talkeetna drainages, and lucrative lode deposits in the Hatcher Pass area. The Turnagain Arm gold rush prompted the development of the first settlements of Americans in substantial numbers in the Cook Inlet area. More than two decades before the founding of Anchorage, two bustling mining camps on Turnagain Arm grew into large towns of several hundred people each. Hope, or Hope City as it was also known, was built at the mouth of Resurrection Creek in 1895 and rapidly became the supply center for the surrounding diggings. The following year, Sunrise City was founded just upstream from the mouth of Sixmile Creek.

These two towns provided the base of operations for the large number of gold seekers, freighters, merchants, saloonkeepers, and wide assortment of gamblers, thieves, prostitutes, and other adventurers who were attracted to every gold rush. Hope and Sunrise also provided shelter for those who "wintered over" between the mining seasons. Sunrise quickly outgrew Hope, reflecting the greater output of gold from Canyon, Mills, Lynx, and Gulch creeks in the Sixmile drainage. Hope remained a dry community for many years. The presence of two saloons in Sunrise may have had something to do with Sunrise's rapid growth in its early years.

As hand mining activity declined and most miners departed, the populations of Sunrise and Hope dwindled. By the summer of 1897, only 80 people were left in Hope and 150 in Sunrise. During the summer of 1898, the population of Sunrise swelled to around 800 people, briefly making it the largest town in the territory. Within a short time, people began leaving in large numbers, signaling the end of the boom. After 1900, the population of Sunrise declined faster than Hope. Several fires destroyed a number of the buildings in Sunrise, and the last trading post closed in 1910. The few miners who remained used the abandoned buildings for firewood. By the 1930s, only two people continued to reside in Sunrise. A small but stable number of people continued to live in Hope, due in part to its more favorable location. Sunrise became a ghost town, and is now a pasture for horses. All that remains of this once thriving mining town along the eroded banks of the Sixmile Creek are faint outlines of the structural foundations and root cellars of some of the former buildings and the ruins of a cabin constructed in the 1930s.

Morgan's reminiscences of his experiences during the Turnagain Arm gold rush provide a rich look into the early years of Sunrise and the experiences of thousands of gold seekers who flocked to Cook Inlet country. In some respects, Morgan's experiences were similar to other latecomers in that he had to work for wages and eventually left to seek his fortune elsewhere. In other respects, his experiences were different, reflecting his abilities and character. He stayed on longer than most - five seasons - and worked for himself during most of that time. He brought money with him, and invested it wisely on a claim on which he had worked as a laborer. He kept an eye out for new prospects, staking additional placer claims on Lynx and other creeks, and several lode claims on tributaries of upper Canyon Creek. Morgan loved the wild country and chose, unlike most, to spend several winters in Sunrise. He also brought his bride to Alaska, a rough country where there were few women and many hardships. Unlike many of his contemporaries, he did not drink or gamble away what he earned. He left Alaska with more in his pocket than he had when he arrived.

The memoirs of A. J. Morgan are important for the insight they provide into the day-to-day life in the mining camps of Turnagain Arm. They also bring to life the colorful personalities of some of the people involved in the district's early history. His recollections provide details about the social interactions between those living in the remote mining camps and the towns of Sunrise and Hope. His experiences illustrate the transition from hand mining techniques to hydraulic mining, and help chronicle the development of Sunrise as a community. In addition to telling a good story, Morgan was an astute observer of human nature. His descriptions of men and women in the mining camps and gold fields of Turnagain Arm illustrate the rich diversity of backgrounds, character traits, and personalities of the people he met and with whom he worked.

Sunrise, Alaska, 1904.
F. H. Moffit, #196, U. S. Geological Survey, Denver, Colorado.

Morgan's own character is a study in contrasts. His gentle sense of humor, the hallmark of his style as a storyteller, contrasts sharply with elements of his character as described by members of his family. By all accounts, Morgan was a pious and proper man. He grew up as a North Carolinian mountain boy, who loved the outdoors. As the son of a southern preacher, he had the temperament and values of a hard-shelled Southern conservative. One of Morgan's grandsons, John Signor, described him as a quiet and soft spoken man, always the gentleman, who could also be bullheaded and autocratic. Unfailingly polite to everyone, Morgan mined in Arizona's toughest gold camp in the 1880s, bossed wild and unruly logging crews in Washington State in the 1890s, participated in the Turnagain Arm gold rush in Alaska from 1897 to 1901, and cruised timber in the rugged conifer forests of the Oregon and Washington coastal mountains for nearly fifty years after the turn of the century. In Alaska, Morgan and his wife filed claims for others, acting as agents for miners who could not read and write. He was genuinely concerned about others, but not given to being pushed around. He considered bragging about one's own deeds, particularly fighting, to be distasteful.

Born in 1868, Morgan grew up in North Carolina during hard times. He left home at age sixteen after his mother was killed in a wagon accident for which he was blamed. He left Franklin with about two dollars in silver, a large clasp knife, and an old Spiller & Burr 36-caliber cap and ball pistol. By the time he reached Atlanta, Georgia, he was riding a mule and had a pack and bedroll. While in Atlanta, he wrote his family that some rough fellows tried to rob him at gun point in the city. According to how one family member recalled the outcome of that encounter, "They didn't have much luck with Jack. He was stubborn about things like that."

In the following years, Morgan made his way across the west working on the railroad. He stopped in places such as Nashville, Oklahoma, and the Texas Panhandle. He described the "boomers" that he encountered in these places as a drunken and rowdy lot. He moved on to the White Mountains of New Mexico, and then to Arizona where he had his first experiences mining for gold in the Tombstone region. After working for other miners, he acquired several mining properties near Tombstone and in the Superstition Mountains near present-day Phoenix. He held these claims until the late 1930s, when he sold them to a large mining corporation. While living in Arizona in the late 1880s, Morgan packed a silver Remington pistol which he used to ward off claim jumpers. He also knew a number of people who became prominent, such as Wyatt Earp, whom Morgan once described as not only a marshal but "a saloonkeeper, cardsharp and whoremaster."

Like many others who grew up on the western American frontier, Morgan had little faith in the justice system. Where he came from, people took care of their own problems. He would not tolerate anyone taking liberties with him or his family. He always kept a loaded firearm close at hand, whether he was mining, logging, traveling, or at home. He is said to have brandished his pistol effectively on more than one occasion when men tried to run him off his mining claims in Arizona and Alaska. While he was not one to look for trouble, he was also not given to backing down. On the frontier experienced by A. W. Morgan, justice was dispensed quickly, with few formalities and little fanfare.

Rumors and stories abound within his family about this quiet but colorful man of action. Parts of his personal history remain shrouded, due in large part to his lifelong refusal to speak of his own deeds. Beginning with his departure as a teenager from the Civil War-ravaged North Carolina, stories have emerged

A. W. "Jack" Morgan, August 24, 1898.

PHOTO COURTESY OF DAVID DUVALL.

from distant relatives and friends about violent encounters with Indians, thieves, claim jumpers, and others of questionable character. One of his Alaskan friends once kidded him about a fight in Alaska in which Morgan allegedly bit off the nose of his antagonist.

A.W. "Jack" Morgan, circa 1910.
PHOTOGRAPH COURTESY OF DAVID DUVALL.

"Jack," as his friends called him, merely smiled at his friend and replied that he could not recall if he spit out the nose after the fight. That was typical of his sense of humor and the off-hand manner in which he ducked queries about past deeds.

Morgan is reported to have killed at least one man and possibly others with his bare hands or a gun. According to a story told by his friend John J. "Jerry" O'Dale in the 1940s, Morgan picked up the nickname "Blackie" or "Black Jack" Morgan in Alaska following an altercation with a drunken miner in Sunrise. The man mistook Morgan's young wife, Lovicia, for one of the prostitutes in Sunrise and laid hands on her. Morgan hit the man so hard that he broke the man's neck. The general consensus of the witnesses, according to O'Dale, was that "the drunken fool had it coming and nothing ever came of it." In later years, Lovicia confirmed that the incident had occurred, but Jack warded off inquiries with the terse comment: "We don't discuss the matter." Stories of other violent encounters with men who tried to take advantage of him have also surfaced over the years. In his later years, after he retired, Morgan is reported to have fatally shot a burglar who had the misfortune to break into his home. These stories, which are difficult to confirm, contribute an air of mystery to his character. They also contrast sharply with the gentle style of storyteller that characterizes his memoirs.

Tall, strong and handsome, Morgan moved easily for a man six feet tall and weighing 195 pounds. He had a boyish face which made him appear younger than his years. He also had a reputation as a charmer and a lady's man. His physical stature and quiet manner contrasted sharply with that of the much younger woman he married and brought to Alaska in 1898. Lovicia Stratton, the sister of his close friend Tom Stratton, was a tiny, strikingly attractive woman of Irish descent. Although petite, she had a very strong personality and could be very outspoken. One family member described her as being "as Irish as could be!" While living in Alaska, Lovicia once routed a black bear with a broom when it tried to raid the cabin on Lynx Creek for bacon and sugar.

Given the sharp contrast in their appearance and personalities, Jack and Lovicia made quite a pair. They shared a sometimes turbulent relationship that spanned more than five decades. Although they later raised two sons, Joseph L. and James D. Morgan, and a daughter, Rebecca Morgan Signor, there was reportedly a chill in their relationship that never healed after the death of their first-born son in Sunrise. Morgan makes few references to his wife in his memoirs about Alaska. There is also no mention of the untimely death of their first-born infant, who is buried at the Point Comfort cemetery at Sunrise. These omissions reflected Morgan's reticence to discuss personal deeds and family matters.

Morgan arrived in the Pacific Northwest from Arizona in 1888. He worked in construction for the Oregon Pacific Railroad at Albany, and then in logging camps at Riddle and Coos Bay, Oregon, and Willapa, Washington. After his Alaskan sojourn, he returned to Washington State where he resumed working as a small scale independent logger. In 1904, he started working in the Willapa Bay-Gray's Harbor area as a timber cruiser, estimating the quality, quantity, and value of uncut timber. A few years later, he moved his family to the Siletz River area in southern Oregon, then to Portland in 1914. He became a timber broker, arranging the sale of tracts of uncut timber for a fee or commission, for various logging companies.

A. W. "Jack" Morgan and Lovicia Morgan, 1910.
Photograph courtesy of David Duvall.

He was highly respected in the timber industry. Millions of dollars changed hands on the basis of his estimates of the amount and quality of timber located on numerous tracts of land. He was subpoenaed as one of the government's witnesses in the timber scandal trials of the 1920s. Morgan was the driving force behind the creation and development of the Lincoln County Fire Patrol. He was also one of the experts called in to help Tillamook and Yamhill County officials organize a fire patrol and reforestation program following the Tillamook Burn fire in 1933, Oregon's greatest timber fire which burned 311,000 acres. His successful career in the logging industry of the Pacific Northwest, which ended with his retirement in 1951, spanned half of a century.

Over the years, many of Morgan's character traits became more pronounced. He never obtained a license to drive and shunned driving automobiles. He reportedly had a bad experience the first time he tried to operate one, and he had no wish to repeat it. As he would say, he did not understand automobiles and he never liked them. He walked whenever possible. When that was not practical, he took the bus or caught rides with friends or relatives. He had a strong distaste for certain forms of mechanization, even as they transformed the world around him. He ran one of the last oxen powered logging operations in the Pacific Northwest.

He quit logging after the turn of the century shortly after the introduction of steam donkeys transformed logging operations.

At middle age, Morgan lost his hearing and had to wear a hearing aid. In his later years, he was given to loudly singing hymns around the house, even though he was not a religious man and did not attend church. He took pride in his membership in the Masonic Lodge, and he was a staunch conservative. Over the years, he had a hearty disdain for Democrats, which he considered the lowest form of political life. His strongest cusswords were "Franklin Delano Roosevelt."

Even in his later years, Morgan was enormously strong and active. On one occasion when he was in his eighties, he took one of his grandsons along on an 18-mile day hike through heavy timber and brush to show a surveyor where a property corner was on one of the timber holdings of the William E. Boeing Company. At the end of the long and exhausting day, the surveyor was suprised to learn that Jack was in his eighties. Morgan continued to be an avid outdoorsman and had remarkable skill with firearms. He kept a loaded pistol in his roll top desk or carried it in his "grip" when he was away from home. He remained a fine pistol shot until his eyes started fading in his late eighties.

A. W. Morgan was known in his family as the "Bull of the Woods." His wife sometimes referred to him as a bull in a china shop because of his penchant for using an axe to fix everything. His children perceived him as a stubborn and dictatorial father, and also as intelligent, patient, and fair with nearly everyone. When his daughter's husband died, she and her two teenaged sons moved into the Morgan household. Jack Morgan was an excellent teacher of the skills he knew best. He taught his grandsons to hunt, shoot, fish, handle an axe and cross-cut saw, and row a boat with a minimum of effort.

During his later years, children, dogs, and fishing were Morgan's weaknesses. He carried an old fashioned snap purse for his pocket change. He entertained children by "majicking" their pennies into more pennies or even nickels and dimes if he was short of pennies. Neighbor children received the same generosity as his grandchildren. Dogs took to him and few strays passed without receiving a handout. Fishing was his main diversion, and he would drop almost any project for a good fishing trip. Morgan was beloved by his family and friends. They will long remember him for the affection that he showered on children and animals, and for his willingness to help friends and neighbors.

Morgan wrote his Alaskan memoirs in bits and pieces over several decades. At the behest of family members, he finally completed them in 1959 when he was in his early nineties. He wrote the final version on an old "Olivera" typewriter, pecking one key at a time, working in his grandson John's bedroom.

In composing his memoirs, Morgan occasionally referred to handwritten, leather-bound calendar diaries that he kept throughout the years. The diaries from his years in Alaska and the following three decades have disappeared. After he passed away in 1964, his grandson, Robert Morgan, had the manuscript retyped, making only a few grammatical corrections.

A. W. "Jack" Morgan, circa 1930.
PHOTOGRAPH COURTESY OF JOHN SIGNOR.

As editor, I made some changes to the manuscript without changing the style or substance of Morgan's writing. The original manuscript had four untitled chapters. I divided each chapter by natural subjects, so the manuscript now has twelve chapters. I also gave each chapter a title drawn from the events described therein. Some of the paragraphs in the original manuscript ran a page or more in length. I divided many long paragraphs to make the narrative more readable. I corrected a few grammatical errors and revised the punctuation to make it consistent. At the beginning of several chapters, I added part of a sentence to provide a better transition between chapters. In about a dozen places I added a word to clarify the meaning of a sentence. I have also attempted in the narrative to identify the full name of as many as possible of the individuals as they appear in official mining records or other documents from the time period. Due to the length of time between the events and the writing of the manuscript, Morgan could not recall the full names of many of the people he met or how to spell their names.

Morgan's simple prose and straightforward style have been retained. For it is his own words that most effectively tell this compelling story of life on one of Alaska's early mining frontiers.

FOREWORD TO SECOND PRINTING

In the fifteen years since *Memories of Old Sunrise* was first published, no new information has surfaced about Jack Morgan and his adventures in Alaska during the Turnagain Arm gold rush. However, several previously unpublished photographs of Jack and Lovicia Morgan have come to light, including the photograph below. Taken in the winter of 1898, the photograph shows them standing at left in front of John Renner's cabin. Also shown in the photograph, standing next to Jack Morgan (from left to right), is Ferdinand Martin, Lewis Shell and his mother Polly Renner, and John Renner. The two men on the far right are unidentified. Jack and Lovicia Morgan maintained contact in later years with many of the people they met at Sunrise. These early gold rush era miners may not have stayed in Alaska, but they treasured the friendships they made and the memories of their years in Cook Inlet Country.

Rolfe Buzzell
Anchorage, Alaska
January 15, 2013

SYDNEY SHELL COLLECTION, COURTESY OF THE SHELL FAMILY, ANCHORAGE.

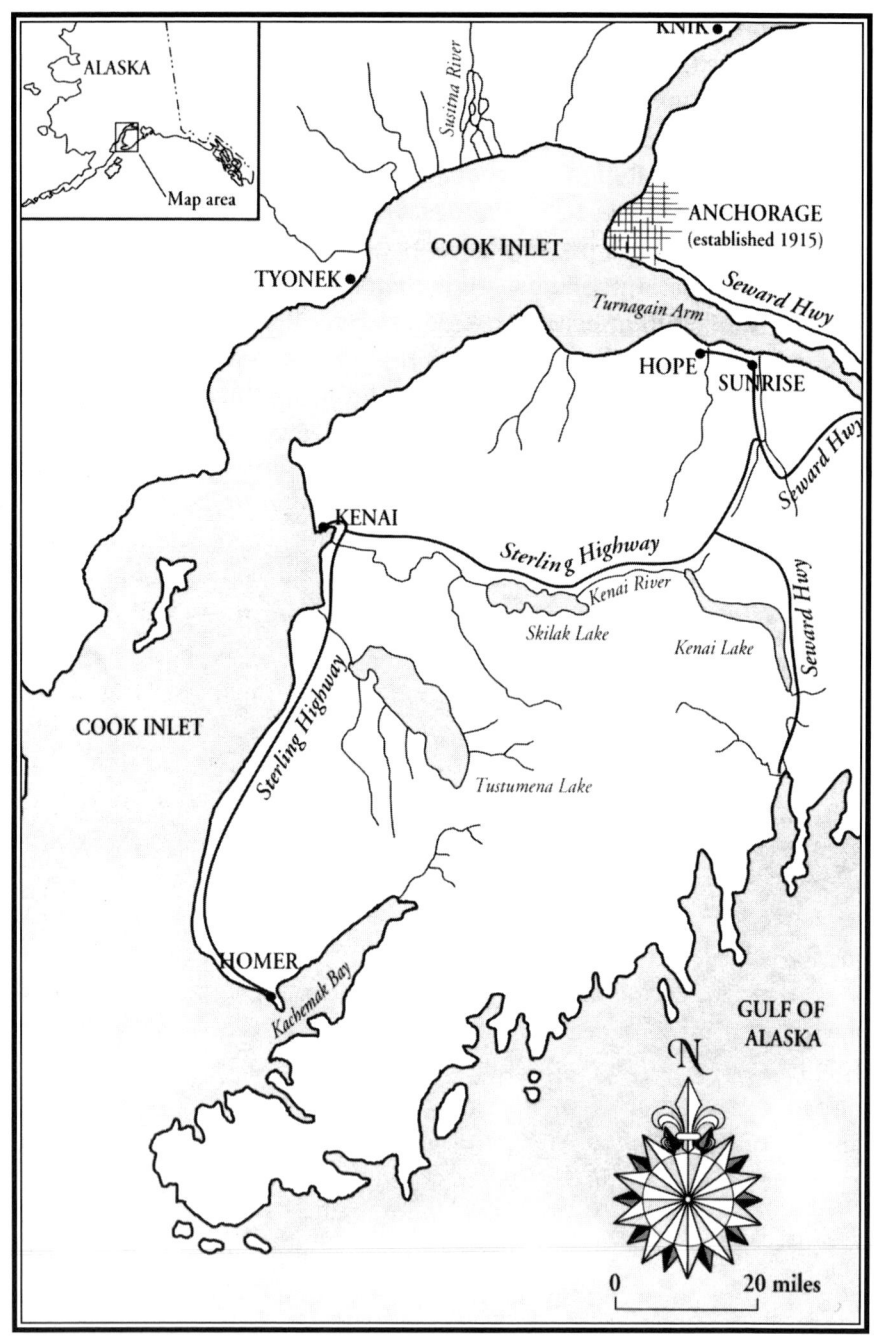

Map of the Kenai Peninsula, Cook Inlet, and Turnagain Arm, Alaska Territory, 1897.
The present-day Seward and Sterling highways were built in the late 1940s.

CHAPTER 1

GOLD FEVER AND A JOURNEY UP THE SUSITNA

The spring of 1897 was getting along toward the tail end of the depression then known as Cleveland hard times. I was in the State of Washington, and had been putting a few logs in the Willapa River, what they would now call "gippoing," with [Thomas] Tom Stratton and Dunk [W.] Bush. As logs were then only four dollars a thousand, one had to work very hard to make even a living. When the news came of the gold strike on the Klondike we were eager to hear more. One man brought out a ton of gold, which excited most everyone, and we talked of going up there.

Bush went over to Aberdeen for some reason and ran into old Doctor Herd over there, who told him that he had been to the Cook Inlet country in Alaska the year before. He told Bush that he and his son made a trip up the Susitna River and discovered some very rich placer ground up there. It was too late in the season to even stake it, as he had to get back to Aberdeen. At Tyonek he had left the boat with his son who was to get things ready to go back next spring and stake and work the ground. He said the top gravel panned five cents to the pan and that there were several rich creeks there.

The doctor wanted a few good men to put up money for an outfit, the freight, and to pay his fare as well as their own so they could go in and work together, share and share alike. Bush said that the people he talked to said the old doctor was reliable.

Old Uncle Johnny Wood, who had built the Simpson Mill at South Bend, Washington, and was living there at Willapa, got the gold fever when all the boats were bringing miners "loaded with gold", so the newspapers stated. He went over to Aberdeen and talked to Doctor Herd, and he was convinced that the old doctor was all right, and that we should go with him.

We did not get the logs rafted and sold until sometime in June, but Bush and Wood were raring to go. They wanted Tom Stratton and me to go with them. When we got to Seattle, there were only two men with him, but they seemed to be nice fellows. Ryan was a real estate man, and Mr. Clay was just a worker like we were.

We discussed the matter with them, and they both thought it was a wonderful opportunity to get in on the ground floor of a mighty good thing. The doctor was a nice looking, quiet man. In trying to size him up, I decided that he should know that if he took six men up there and they found he had not been up there before, nor found the ground to be as he had claimed, he might not come back. And so I told him. We dug up the money to buy a big supply of groceries—enough, we thought, to keep us all summer—and all kinds of mining tools: shovels, picks, gold pans, a whipsaw, and small tools that would be needed. We bought the doctor a ticket to Tyonek, and tickets for ourselves, which ran into considerable money, but I do not remember now how much each of us had to put up.

We sailed on an old tub called the *Mexico*, and had to go steerage, as all the cabins had been taken before we got there. This boat went as far as Juneau, where we changed onto the Alaska Commercial Company's boat the *Bertha*. It was also loaded down with men going back to their mines, and we were again crowded into the steerage.

It made no difference to me, as I was seasick all the way to the mouth of Cook Inlet. The other boys talked to a number of miners on their way back to their mines who did not believe that the old doctor had ever been up the river as he claimed, and that there had ever been any gold discovered on the Susitna River, or any of the streams coming in to the west side of Cook Inlet.

Of course this was certainly disconcerting, but no one said much. When we got to Tyonek, neither the doctor's son nor the boat were there. However, the doctor said he would buy a boat, which he did. But Bush, Wood, and Tom were disgusted and said they would go instead to the Turnagain Arm country, as they heard there were some paying placer mines at Hope and Sunrise, and that they could no doubt get jobs in the mines, and also lease ground to work. We had bought two good tents and two Yukon stoves, so they proposed to divide the outfit and separate.

I thought that it might be a good idea to go up this big river, the Susitna, as it was all vacant and there might be some rich creeks up there. I did not know then that it was a big flat valley, but found out later. So I stayed with the doctor and his friends. My friends were glad to have me go, as I took power of attorney to locate claims for them if we found any good ground. They got on the little steamer *Perry* and left for the [Turnagain] Arm.

The next day we loaded our outfit into the big dory that the doctor bought and started up the [Cook] Inlet toward the Susitna. We got a late start and the tide turned on us at the mouth of the Beluga River, and we camped there that night. We had to unload the boat and carry everything up on the high bank, as the tide rose away up there. I will not forget that camp, as Uncle Johnny Wood had brought along two old single shot Winchester rifles and cartridges. He had loaned me one, as he said there should be lots of game where we were going. Clay and I put our blanket rolls together and slept together, and I had the rifle lying beside me. There was a little pond of water about fifty yards from our beds. Alongabout nine or ten o'clock two geese flew over us very low and lit in the pond.

Tyonek, 1898. The tents of prospectors are on the beach on the left.
W. C. Mendenhall #15, U. S. Geological Survey, Denver, Colorado.

I said to Clay: "I can still see the sights on the gun and maybe I can shoot one's head off, so we can have a goose for tomorrow."

I did not get up, just lay there and shot, and we saw the goose flop out its wings and settle down. I pulled on my gum boots, and went out and found the two of them sitting there with their necks broken. They happened to be just in line, something that might not happen again in a thousand years.

We loaded our boat and started up on the tide next morning, expecting to get into the river early, but got only a few miles up the Inlet when a wind came up, they said from Turnagain Arm. Clay and I were at the oars, with Ryan steering, when the water got so rough that it was rolling into the boat. Ryan decided we had better beach the boat and save what we could of our stuff before we swamped. So he headed for the shore. The spray was flying so that we could not see anything, but the Lord must have been with us, as we ran into a little slough about forty feet wide and shot around a bend into still water.

The doctor had learned something about the country, as he said that the wind would blow for three days, and that we would have to put up our tent and get our stuff into it. We had a tent frame, and it took the four of us a long time to get the tent stretched and pegged down so it would not blow away. It was a big, flat country littered with driftwood, and I imagine that, at extreme high tides, the water came over the ground where we were. We had plenty of wood for the stove. The water was not real salty, but what they called brackish. The only way we could drink it was to make it very strong with tea or coffee. There were thousands of geese and ducks feeding on the grassy flat, but the wind was blowing so hard that no one could see to shoot. In fact, we did not need meat at that time.

I think that was the most miserable three days that I ever put in. I had a good, heavy canvas around my blanket roll, but the cold would come up through the canvas and the blankets so that one side of me would get so cold I had to roll over, and then the other side would feel like I was freezing before I could get to sleep. The third morning the wind quit, and the sun came out and it was good old summertime again. The tide was running up when we loaded our stuff in the boat, and we were happy to be on our way early. We got into the river and soon met a good current coming down. Two men with the oars could make slow headway against the current, and we could take advantage occasionally of the eddies. Finally we ran into long, swift riffles, but had anticipated this and had brought a hundred and fifty feet of half inch rope. There is usually a gravel bar alongside swift riffles. Ryan, Clay, and I would pull on the rope from the bar while the doctor sat in the stern with an oar and kept the boat from hitting the bank. We worried along this way until about six o'clock, when I was glad to hear Mr. Clay say: "Alaska, here we rest."

There was a nice gravel bar to camp on, and we did not have to unload the boat or put up the tent, just cooked a good dinner, spread our beds on the soft sand, and made up for sleep we lost down on the flat.

The sun was way up when we got up next morning. When Ryan tried to get up he groaned, and fell back in the bed with a bad attack of lumbago. The doctor asked him how long the attacks lasted when they came, and he said about two weeks. We talked it over, and decided we had better go back. I then asked how far the doctor thought it was up to where they found the good ground. He studied awhile and said he did not know, but thought it was quite a way. And I then asked him how the river was as to riffles, etc. He hesitated awhile, then said he did not remember much about it. I was sure then that he had never been there at all.

The valley seemed quite wide there, and, as I remember, the terrain rose up gradually toward the Knik country, and there were bunches of cottonwood trees and a few spruce trees scattered among them. The Alaska Commercial Company had a store at Knik, where or near where Anchorage is now. We had the tide with us when we got down in the Inlet, and got to Tyonek along in the afternoon.

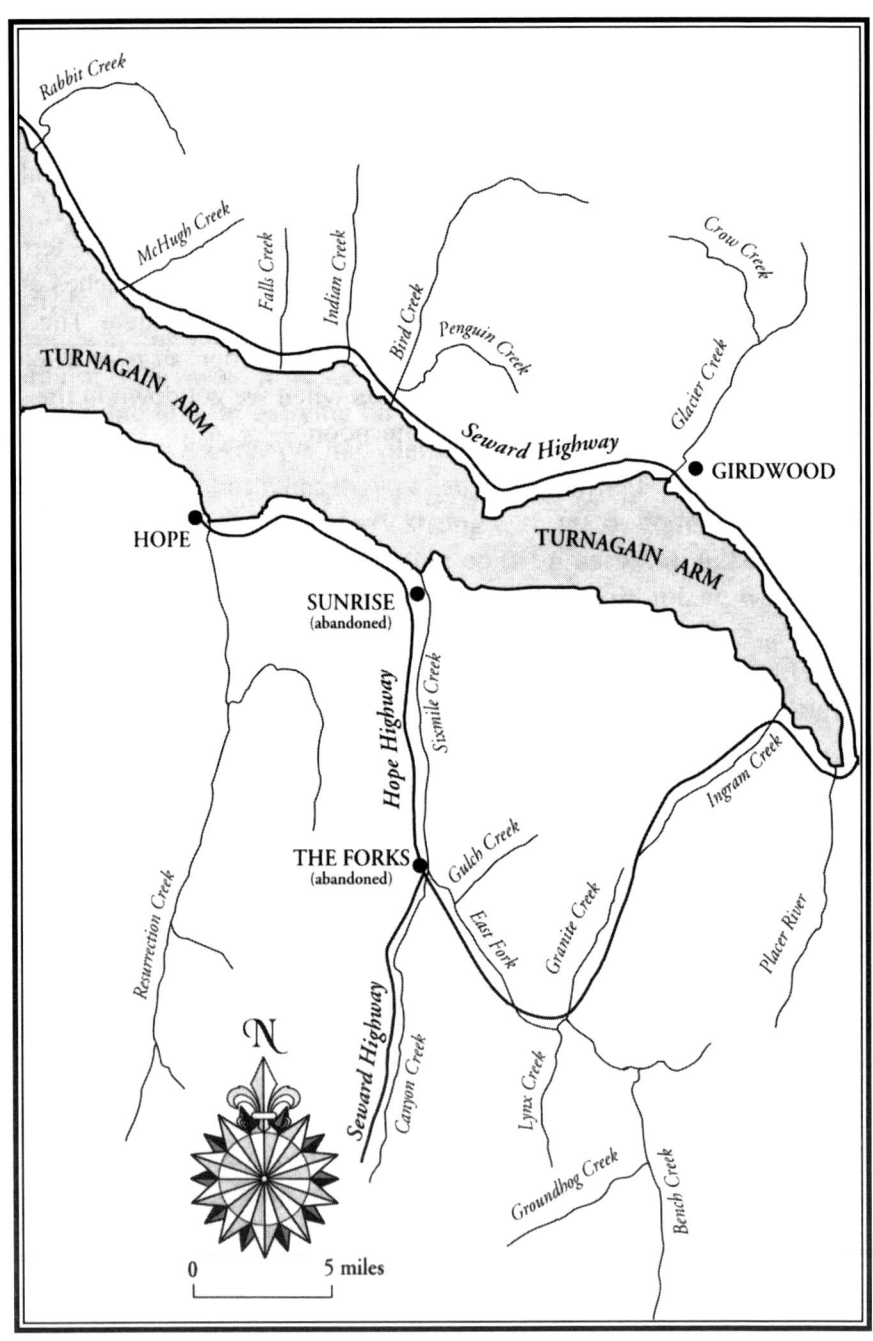

Map of the Turnagain Arm Mining District, 1897, showing locations of present-day Seward and Hope highways.

CHAPTER 2

PROSPECTING ON RESURRECTION AND BIRD CREEKS

About the time we got there the *Perry* was returning from Sunrise. Its skipper, Captain [Austin E.] Lathrop, told us that he had taken our friends to Sunrise, and he was going back on the next tide, so we went with him. It was a fine day, and the little boat glided along with the tide, getting us to Sunrise before the tide turned.

There was a little makeshift wharf where the boats landed. Tom Stratton was standing there on the wharf. When I got off the boat I saw a man standing on the other side of the wharf who I thought was Tom Creason, a man I had worked in camp with on Coos Bay, Oregon, during the summer of 1890.

I said to Tom: "Is that man's name Creason?"

He said: "Yes, he's building a store here for the Alaska Commercial Company, and I am working for him."

The L. J. Perry (on the left) and two other unidentified vessels at Hope, 1898.
JOHN BROOKS COLLECTION, UNIVERSITY OF ALASKA FAIRBANKS.

So I walked over and stuck out my hand and said: "Hello, Tom. What are you doing away up here?"

He laughed and shook hands, and said: "I guess you must know my brother Tom Creason."

I had worked with Tom Creason in a logging camp. He and his brother, Al, did look very much alike.

Tom Stratton said that Bush and Johnny Wood had gone to Hope to look at some ground that the owner wanted to lease. We got our stuff off the *Perry* and divided it, as I was going to move into the tent with Tom Stratton, Johnny Wood, and Bush. Bush came back from Hope that night. He reported that Johnny Wood and another man had leased a worked-out claim on Bear Creek, but he did not believe they could make wages on it. The main channel had been worked out, and there were just a few rims left that had any gold in them. He was right, as poor old Johnny just made a little more than his fare back home on the boat that fall for his summer's work.

When Bush returned from Hope, he was very excited as he had run into an old acquaintance named Dunton. This Dunton had lived on a homestead at Smith Creek in Washington, where a man by the name of Charley Lockhart was putting in some logs, and boarding with the Duntons. Apparently Dunton had thought his wife, who was much younger than he was, might think more of Charley than she did of him, and decided that he would kill Charley. Charley and I had bought a forty of timber[1] there on Fairchild Creek and had felled and bucked[2] it. We made a road into the forty. Tom Stratton and Bob Marshall, who had an ox team, were hauling in our logs. Charley was taking care of the landing and keeping the road clear, and I was swamping and barking[3] the logs. Tom was helping me bark and drove the dogs[4] in the logs.

While Marshall was away with a load, we heard several shots down near the landing, and thought that old man Hart, where we boarded, was killing a deer. But as Marshall went down with the next load of logs, he saw Charley's shovel in the middle of the road where he had been putting in a skid. When he came back he wanted to know where Charley was, but we did not know. We were getting

---

1   Forty acres of uncut timber land.

2   Cut the trees down and sawed them into standard log lengths.

3   Knocking off the limbs, cutting a "snipe" or beveled edge at the forward end of the log, and stripping the bark so the logs could be dragged by a team of oxen.

4   "Dogs" were long steel pins driven into opposite sides of the sniped end of a log and chained to an oxen team. The dogs prevented the log from rolling sideways off of the skid road when being pulled in tandem with other logs.

a load ready, but before Bob started with the load, three men came from up the road and asked if we knew where Charley was. They said Dunton went by their place and told them he had killed Charley.

We went down to where the shovel was and I picked up five empty shells from a 45-90 Winchester. Dunton had come up below Charley and started shooting, but apparently the dirt slipped under his feet and he slid down and missed. Of course Charley ran up the road to where he could get in the brush. Dunton kept shooting at him and came close enough one shot to burn a streak clear across his thigh. Charley was really scared by that time. He said he had to climb over a big windfall, and that Dunton got real close and shot just as he fell off the log on the other side. That was when Dunton thought he got him. Charley was in the brush out of sight by the time Dunton got on the windfall, and ran on and hid in a salmonberry patch. We followed Charley's tracks to the salmonberry patch and hollered at him to come out, as Dunton had gone on home thinking he killed him. Charley was very pale, and showed us where one bullet had cut a hole in his pants and underwear, and the red streak around his thigh.

By dinner time that evening he was still so scared he couldn't eat a bite. He told me he was leaving at once, and asked me to finish putting in the logs, sell them, and send his half of the money when I got it. He walked on up to Francis that night and went by train next morning over on the Cowlitz River and got a job in a logging camp.

I suppose that some of Dunton's friends told him that it was surely a penitentiary offense to go on a man's place, shoot at him, and try to kill him. So he too left.

And now Bush had found him living in a good cabin at Hope. Bush said that Dunton showed him a twenty dollar nugget that he said he found on a little creek about twenty miles up Resurrection Creek. He wanted Bush to help him prospect the creek for a half interest, if it was rich enough to work. Bush said it must be all right. He was glad that I had overtaken them so I could go with him, as Dunton did not know me and would not know that I was Charley's partner at the time he tried to shoot Charley. I hesitated about going, but Tom and Bush said: "Oh, go on, he may have a fortune in the little creek."

So Bush and I loaded up a pack of groceries and a bed roll, and we went down to Hope and met Dunton at his cabin. He seemed glad to see us and seemed to be perfectly rational.

He no doubt was glad to see someone from his former home country. From his pleasant way, you would hardly believe that he tried hard to kill my old logging partner. He talked late into the night, and told us of his experiences there at Hope. He had worked summers for old one-eyed [Patrick] Reilly in his Bear Creek placer mine, and during winters hunted moose.

We went up the river toward his creek. Bush and I were loaded down with groceries and tools to use prospecting. Every little while he would point out a place where he had killed a moose. He carried his 45-90 rifle, and said we would likely see a moose and he would shoot it so we would have fresh meat. I did not like the idea of killing a moose just for a few days' feed out of it, but did not say anything as he was boss then. We were going up a partially timbered ridge near his creek when we ran into a lot of fresh moose tracks. Dunton was ahead and turned out in the timber and brush following the moose sign. Bush had dropped behind us and did not see him go into the brush. When he caught up with me, he said: "Where did Moosey go?"

Dunton came out of the brush and could not help hearing it, but said nothing. We soon got up to where this creek came out of a canyon, looked around to see where we should prospect, and made camp. There was no place we could see where he could have found a nugget, and we asked him where he found it. He said he could not locate the place, as he found it in the winter when the snow was on. It then occurred to me that he picked it up on bedrock, when he was working for Reilly.

We ran cuts in the gravel and sank holes to bedrock, as it was shallow, and never got a color. Dunton agreed that there was no use working any longer there and said it might have been on some other little creek he found the nugget. He then suggested that we go back to Hope and go across Turnagain Arm to Bird Creek, as there was gold there. A few mines were working, but mostly were vacant then as most of the men who had staked claims on the creek had not done their last year's assessments. Bush and I discussed the situation, and as we had enough groceries to feed the three of us another week, we decided to go over and at least see Bird Creek. The storekeeper there told us how to go across, and said there was no wind and the Arm was smooth. Dunton also knew what to do and got a good boat to use.

The Arm is supposed to have the second highest tide in the world. In ebbing, it runs almost dry, that is, there is only the fresh water coming down from the river above. When the tide turns it comes in with what they call a bore, with a wave running ten or fifteen feet high, then another one not so high, and the third only a few feet high. Then it's safe to go on it with a boat.

By the time we were ready to leave, the water had got up to Hope so we could get out. We were told to head straight across toward Bird Creek and pull hard until the tide turned. We were up opposite Sunrise when the tide turned and were half across the Arm. We pulled hard, and by the time the tide got down so we could get into Bird Creek we were across. There was water enough in the creek so we could keep the boat afloat and get up to the timber. There we found a good place to camp.

Main Street, Hope Alaska, circa 1906.
Wheatley Collection, Anchorage Museum at Rasmuson Center .

There is around six inches of soft moss on the ground in the timber up there, and it makes a good mattress to sleep on.

We had time to go up further where some Natives from Kodiak were shovelling gravel into sluice boxes. Their boss showed us around and said there was lots of fine gold in the gravel, but he did not believe they were saving all of it. They were not taking good wages out, just enough to live on. He hoped to find it better farther on as they would get deeper into the gravel. We went up to the other outfit and they told us the same story, and said all the creek above them was vacant then.

Dunton still had his old rifle with him, and he had been out in the woods. He said he saw a big moose and tried to shoot it, but his gun snapped, as it had got rusty and the firing pin was stuck. He said he had oiled it so it would work, and he would get a moose next day. We told him that we really did not need one, and that we must get busy and find a place to prospect. There were plenty of moose around, as the ground was cut up with fresh tracks along the trail going up the river. We took a lunch and tools and went up the creek until we found a nice long bar with a swift riffle alongside of it and decided that was the place to run a cut in the bar. In panning we found fine gold right on top, which was encouraging. And as our cut got deeper the colors were heavier. One of us would pan occasionally, and always got a string of colors in the pan.

I was panning one day in the edge of the eddy at the foot of the riffle and saw a splash right up against the pan. I looked up and there was a bunch of big trout milling around, apparently looking for flies on top of the water. I jumped up and asked the boys if they had a fish hook or line in their pockets, and they had none. Then I asked if they had a pin, but none could be found. I happened to have a safety pin, so I straightened it out and made a hook. I took the hardware string I had used to tie up our lunch, tied it [the hook] to the string, and cut a little willow pole. Bush had red flannel underwear, and he cut a little piece from his drawers, which I put on the hook. I cast out, and the trout all came for it. The fastest one got it, and I threw him out on the bar. I kept casting and got one every cast. It kept Bush busy killing them and putting them up until I got all of them. We counted 24, running from 14 to 16 inches, all fat and heavy. I do not know what kind they were, as I never saw any more like them while I was up there. They were a real treat, a welcome change from bacon.

Dunton would go out every day to get us a moose, but did not see any more. We saw that he was not much on the work, and we looked around to see if there was any little creek coming in near the bar to make a sluice head for boxes, and found none. Since we did not believe there was enough gold in the gravel to pay to work it, we decided to leave. There was also that thought that if things did not go to suit Dunton, he might use his old rifle on us as he had on Charley. So we told him we were through, as we did not believe it would pay to work the gravel. He still thought it would, and tried to persuade us to stick to it. When he saw we would not, he was pleasant about it, and went with us to Sunrise in the boat.

CHAPTER 3

PROSPECTING THE SIXMILE DRAINAGE

Bush and I prospected around Sunrise on the river and small creeks where there were a few fellows working, but none of them had struck good pay where they could get at it. Considerable gold had come down Sixmile Creek from The Forks where Canyon Creek and the East Fork come together. Below this, the Sixmile Creek flattens out into a valley from a quarter to a half mile wide, then flows through a canyon for a few miles to Sunrise and the Arm.

Bush decided that everything that was any good had been staked, and that he would try to get a job and make enough to get back home that fall.

When we were in Tyonek we ran into an old fellow who called himself Major [S.] Matson. He had been a very tall man, but was now stooped over. He claimed he was retired from the army, and I think he was getting a pension. He talked to everyone around and told some wonderful tales of his experiences. He came over to Sunrise on the *Perry*, saw our tent and talked to us about the time Bush wanted to go up the trail looking for a job. He told us that there were some good claims on upper Mills Creek that had gone vacant, as the owners did not come back that year. I was still gullible when he wanted me to go with him to prospect and locate them, so I loaded up my bed roll and my pack with enough grub to last him and me about a week. Bush did the same.

We had heavy loads and of course had to rest often. At one stop, Matson told us that he had killed a famous outlaw in Montana and got ten thousand dollars reward for it. I think the outlaw's name was Montana Pete. We got up to The Forks early and made camp above the Rivers Hotel, where they fed people and had a bunkhouse for them to sleep in. It was a very good place to stay, but since we had our cooking outfit, grub, and bedrolls to sleep in, and were saving every dollar we could, we cooked our evening meal. Sam [Sanford J.] Mills, who lived just beyond the hotel, saw our smoke and came down to see who it was. He and the major visited while we were getting the meal. When it was ready we asked Sam to eat with us. He said that he would not eat our food, which we had

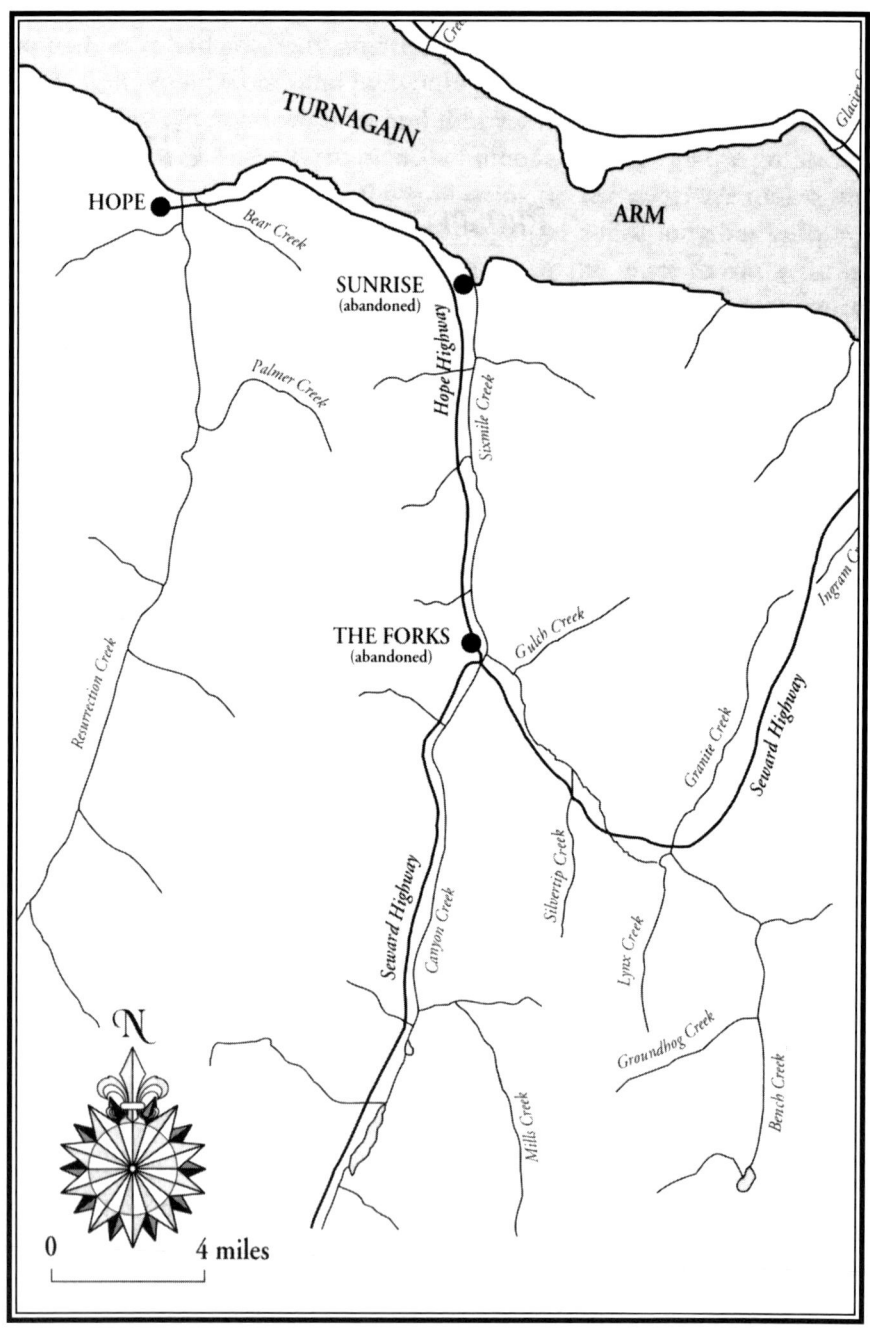

Map of Sixmile drainage, showing location of present-day
Seward and Hope highways.

carried so far on our backs, but would have his supper in his cabin where he had a big moose stew warm on his stove. He promised he would come back later to visit with us awhile.

After he left, the Major said: "Isn't he the biggest liar you ever heard talk?"

After we ate, the Major said he was going down to the lodge and beat [John C.] Rivers out of a cigar shaking the dice. He had not got back when Mills came and said: "Where is the old Major?"

We told him: "He's gone to the lodge to get a cigar."

Then Mills said: "Isn't he the biggest liar you ever heard talk?"

Of course we had to laugh, but did not tell him that the Major asked us the same question about him.

When the Major got back, he and Mills started swapping experiences. They had both been in Montana and both had trapped and scouted with Jim Bridger. They both knew a lot of the same people.

Finally the Major asked Sam: "Did you know this famous outlaw, Montana Pete?"

Sam replied: "I guess I did, I killed the s.o.b. and got ten thousand dollars reward for it."

Bush punched me with his elbow and whispered: "They will be good friends now. They both killed the same man."

Sam told us that Mr. [William "Billy" P.] Powers, who had a claim on Lynx Creek, wanted a man to work for him, so Bush said he would try to get the job. Lynx Creek came into the East Fork ten or twelve miles above The Forks. The Major decided that he wanted to see Lynx Creek, too. This pleased Bush, as he said if we went with him he would go on to Mills Creek with us if he did not get the job with Powers.

Bush got the job, and the Major said we should go on up to see what they were doing on the claims above there. We stopped at all the claims that were being worked, and the boss would come out and show us over his mine. I think they all wanted to sell at their price.

As I remember, we walked back down to The Forks and started on to Mills Creek next morning.

The Major was right, as all of Mills Creek was vacant above [Herman A.] Schmeser's claim. There were five good claims in the canyon of Mills Creek belonging to Clint [Charles E.] Pierce, a Mr. [W. W.] Price, [John] "Jack" Renner, [Robert] Bob Michaelson, and a man named [Albert M.] Brown, all fine men. They had consolidated their claims and formed the Polly Mining Company. Since they were good miners they did well. The first few years they all went outside for the long winters, and I understood that they cleared around fifteen thousand dollars each for a few years. After I got there in 1897, I think they did not take out so much, and so stayed in Alaska during the winters, as they all had good, comfortable cabins in Sunrise.

Mining Camp at "The Forks," where Canyon Creek and East Fork merge into Sixmile Creek.
F. H. Moffit #105, U. S. Geological Survey, Denver, Colorado.

Hans Severson had the first claim above them, and he struck it good the first two years, as the lower end of his claim was partly in the canyon. But when we got up there he was working alone and not finding much gold. Schmeser was not working, as his ground would hardly pay wages. The country flattened out above him, and the gravel was only a few feet deep on it. There was some fine gold in all of it, but not enough to pay to work.

The Major and I made camp. I put down a lot of holes to bedrock and panned the gravel, as there was no gold on bedrock and not much in the gravel. The Major saw it was no good, but thought I should keep on prospecting it as there might be a rich streak somewhere on it. He said he would go out, as he expected a check in the mail, but would come back in a few days and bring more grub. I did not expect him back, but I had packed enough stuff up there to last me a few more days, so I decided to stay. I went further up to camp and had some hope of striking pay on some of the small creeks, but it was all about the same: a little gold in the wash, but not enough to pay to work. I roamed around, however, and saw a lot of the country. There were lots of ptarmigan there. I carried the old single shot Winchester along, and could get close enough to shoot their heads off, so I had ptarmigan every meal.

On my way back to Sunrise, I stopped and visited with Sam Mills for awhile. I told him what I had been doing. He thought I should prospect Walker Creek, as he did not believe anyone had ever prospected it. It was five miles above Sunrise on the opposite side of the river.

When I got back to Sunrise, Tom Stratton told me that if I would stick around a few days until the store building he was working on was finished, he would be out of a job and he would go with me to prospect Walker Creek. He said that Al Creason was then batching upstairs in the store. A Mrs. [Martha] White was staying there while her husband [E. A. White] had gone up the river to look for a job. Creason had a young Copper River Indian staying with him cleaning up and doing such work as was needed around the store. He also brought goods from the wharf to the store on a wheelbarrow.

I had come over to the store and was sitting on the steps when Mrs. White came out on the porch, introduced herself and began telling me her troubles. She and her husband had been working at the Ladd salting plant near Tyonek the last summer. Ladd's plant salted salmon and shipped it to his home town, San Francisco, but the depression had got so bad that he could not sell his salmon. [Charles D.] Ladd had left the Whites in charge of the plant for the winter, but did not come back in the spring, so they had no pay for their year's work, and had to hunt a job now.

While she was talking, the young Indian came up with his wheelbarrow load of goods, which I think he turned over purposely so that he could demonstrate to us that he was learning our language fast. He had learned all the vile words that I had ever heard, and started calling the wheelbarrow all the vile names he could remember. Mrs. White got up and started toward the store door when Creason came out. She told him she could not stand hearing an Indian using vile language.

Creason said: "Was he swearing in your presence?"

She replied: "The vilest language I ever heard."

Then he said: "Grab a club and go down and whale the Jesus out of him."

The next day [J. N.] Johnston arrived. He was traveling with his own boat and had quite a bunch of furs with him. He said he went around to the Indian camps and picked up furs for the Alaska Commercial Company. He told me an interesting story about Creason. He said that Creason had been with the company for around fifteen years, and a few years before that he was with [Thomas W.] Hanmore, the main guy for the company there on the Inlet. They had a store at Knik, near where Anchorage now is.

During the winter some Indians came over to Tyonek and told him that one of the Indians had shot and killed the agent at Knik. Hanmore sent Creason back with them to take over the store and handle the matter the best he could. When Creason got over there he buried the dead agent with the help of the Indians, and told them to bring in the man that killed him. The Indians said he had gone over into the Copper River country, and they could not get him. Creason told them they would have to get him and bring him in, or they could not get anything to eat from the store. They hung out a few days, and Creason would not let them even come into the store. So they went over and brought in the Indian.

Creason had a gallows ready to hang him on, but held a trial. Creason was the judge, and called witnesses who saw the Indian shoot the agent. He found the Indian guilty of murder, and sentenced him to hang by his neck until he was dead.

He ordered the other Indians to put a rope around the Indian's neck and stand him on a box under the gallows, and then kick the box from under him. The Indians refused, and Creason had to do it himself. He let him hang in front of the store all day while he sold food to the Indians. He told the Indians to take the hanging man down and bury him near where the agent was buried. Creason read the funeral service for him the same as he had for the agent. Johnston said the Indians had a lot of respect for Creason after this. I never asked Creason anything about it, as I imagined he would not care to talk about it. I learned from others who were there at the same time that this is the true story.

I had scouted around and found a way to get across the Sixmile Creek and up to Walker Creek. So when Tom was laid off, we made packs of groceries and a cooking outfit, took shovels and a pick and went up to where the creek came out of the canyon onto the flat that extended to the river about a quarter of a mile. We made our camp here. On the other side of the creek there was a shelving rock. The water rushing out of the canyon whirled around under it, and every few minutes would make a noise like people talking. At first we would look up to see who was coming. When we learned that it was the water producing human voices, we said we would change the name of the creek and call it Talking Creek.

We could get fine colors on the flat, but not very much. The water was so high in the canyon that the only thing we could do was to gouge in along the rim and get some of the loose, soft rim rock to pan. This panned well, as we would get coarse gold in every pan and even got one little nugget worth almost a dollar. It was a shale formation, and we thought if there was that much gold along the rim it ought to be good down in the channel which was not very wide. We could not figure out any way to work it while the creek was so high. So we measured off three claims and staked them. We had them recorded as we went up by The Forks where Sam Mills was recorder for the district.

We decided to go up the East Fork to see what was up there. If we did not find anything better, we would come back to Walker Creek late in the fall and try to get down in the channel. Everyone we met would stop us to talk and give us advice as to where to go to prospect.

On this trip we met an old fellow named [H. P.] Walker who was sick with awful pains in his liver. He was sure [he knew] what was wrong, as he said he got his liver frozen during the winter when he was out moose hunting. We knew that Walker must have gall stones, but did not say anything, as we did not want to spoil his story about getting his liver frozen. He said his brother was coming in on the next boat to take him to a doctor. They had a claim on Gulch Creek that emptied into East Fork about a mile above The Forks. There were a few claims on this little creek that were fairly good, but they were shallow and were worked out fast.

Knik, Alaska.
WHEATLEY COLLECTION, ANCHORAGE MUSEUM AT RASMUSON CENTER.

There were a few fellows working on it then. The Goetz brothers leased the Walker claim and worked on it several years. The Walker brothers went out on the next boat and neither of them came back.

As I think back over the years spent in Sunrise, I remember a number of characters who were given nicknames like "Long Shorty," who was around six feet seven inches. As I recall, his real name was Palmer. Another one was "Moose Anchor Bill." His real name was Bill Darr.

The first winter at Hope, someone killed several moose a few miles up the river from Hope, and told everyone there to go and get the meat they wanted. When they got loaded up, there was a young moose left, and this Bill said he could sled it in alone. They advised him he should take half of it and come back and get the other half. But he was afraid someone else would come and get it, so he put it all on his sled, but was able to pull it only a short way. When the others got back to Hope they [were] asked where Bill was. They said they had left him anchored to a moose. He was always Moose Anchor Bill afterward.

Tom and I went on up past the mouth of Lynx Creek and found a good trail to the mouth of a little creek called Groundhog Creek. Charley Mason had taken a claim there and done considerable work. He had his boxes piled up[1], as apparently he could not make wages working the ground and had gone over to Canyon or Mills Creek to work in some of the mines there. We panned around his cuts and could get colors every pan, but they were fine. From there on we had to cut a lot of brush to make a trail to get through. As I remember it was six or seven miles from there to the real head of the East Fork. There was a beautiful little lake about a mile long in a low pass between East Fork and Johnson Creek that ran the other way and emptied into Kenai Lake. There were some little creeks emptying into the lake which drained into East Fork, but as I remember now it would not have taken much work to lower the other end so the lake would go to the Kenai side. There was a fine waterfall just beyond the end of the lake and a rock bluff full of quartz stringers. We dug holes and panned all around there but never got a color. We had got above the gold spill.

We went back down and crossed over to Granite Creek, into nice country, as it was a wide flat. The creek emptied into East Fork on the opposite side from Lynx Creek. It was still in the gold belt, as we could get a string of fine colors in every pan. It had all been staked, however, and showed some work on some of the claims. The owners had evidently not found enough gold to pay, had piled up their boxes and no doubt gone to work for wages in other mines. We went on down to Silvertip

---

1   Removal of the sluice boxes from the creek bed so they would not be damaged by flooding or freeze up.

Creek where there was a cabin, but it too, was deserted. We panned there and got colors in every pan, but the owners no doubt could not make it pay. We were out of grub then, and went on to Sunrise, not knowing where to look next.

Mining camp at Groundhog Creek.
PHOTOGRAPH COURTESY OF THE ANCHORAGE MUSEUM AT RASMUSON CENTER.

When we got to Sunrise, we found Dunton waiting for us. He had gotten help, had made boxes, and had cleaned up considerable gold. But it was maybe not enough to pay wages, and he wanted us to go with him to help work it. Old Major Matson came over on a little schooner that brought goods from Seattle for the U. S. Mercantile Company store. Tom saw the captain, who was going to start back in a day or so, and arranged to go back with him. He said he had seen all of "Alasky" that he wanted to see. We found a letter from Bush saying that Powers needed another man and would give one of us a job if we would go up. Bush said he liked the work there.

Tom said: "You get up there as quick as you can and get to work. You fiddled away too much time trying to find something for yourself. It's just not here."

Dunton and the Major both stayed in our tent and had supper with us, and slept there that night, or tried to. Dunton gritted his teeth when asleep, and he could be heard fifty yards away. I had got used to it while out with him and Bush, but the Major and Tom could not sleep much. The Major got up sometime in the night and went up to the hotel.

When we were getting up the next morning, Dunton woke up and looked around and asked: "Where is the old Major?"

Tom said: "I think the old s.o.b. has gone to find a grindstone to grind his teeth, as he was whetting them all night long."

I kicked Tom's foot, and he realized then that it was Dunton who was whetting his teeth. Tom's face got red, but Dunton did not say anything. He tried again to get me to go to Bird Creek with him, but I told him I had a job then and was going to take it.

Tom gathered up his things, took them down and put them on the boat, and left for Washington. Ryan left too, and Dr. Herd and Clay went out later. This left only me out of the boys who had come up with old Dr. Herd. I shook the old Major and packed up what I would need to go to Lynx Creek. It made a big load. I had the pack train take my bedding, as it was leaving for Lynx Creek that day, but I carried more than a hundred pounds. I traveled slowly, and stayed at The Forks that night. I went on up to Lynx Creek the next day.

CHAPTER 4

MINING AT LYNX CREEK

When I got up to the Powers claim, Powers came out, took one look at my pack, then tried to lift it.

He asked: "My God, boy, did you carry it all the way from Sunrise? That must weigh a hundred and fifty pounds."

Bush was glad to see me, and I moved in the tent with him. We had a little stove to cook on, and found plenty of grass to make a mattress to sleep on. Two other men were working there. Powers had taken out some money the year before, and had gone down to Sitka to winter after it froze up. Apparently he got acquainted with the Ranzona boys [brothers Phil E. and A. B. Ranzona] who had a saloon there. He got into a poker game, lost his stake, and owed the Ranzonas fifteen hundred dollars when it was time to go back in the spring. He told them about his claim and gave them a third interest in it to settle his debt and get money enough to go back on.

Phil, the youngest boy, went back into the Arm with Powers to help work the claim. He could not do much, and Powers did not seem to work very hard, as he was boss. They had run a cut at the lower end of the claim, but it was about fifteen feet to bedrock there, and they could not make wage shoveling it. He then had moved up about half way, and started another cut. When I arrived he had got to bedrock in the channel.

Bush was a good worker, who could do as much as two ordinary men. We moved along very good and were getting in good pay. Powers cleaned up often and he seemed to take an interest in showing Bush and me how to clean up. I had not been there very long when Powers took the gold that he had cleaned up to town and said he would order a lot of stuff and be back in a couple of days. Phil Ranzona was trying to sell his interest, but no one seemed to want it.

Phil had a streak of humor in him. One day one of the boys from up the creek came along and asked: "Phil, how are you coming?"

Phil said: "Fine. I made fifteen hundred dollars this morning."

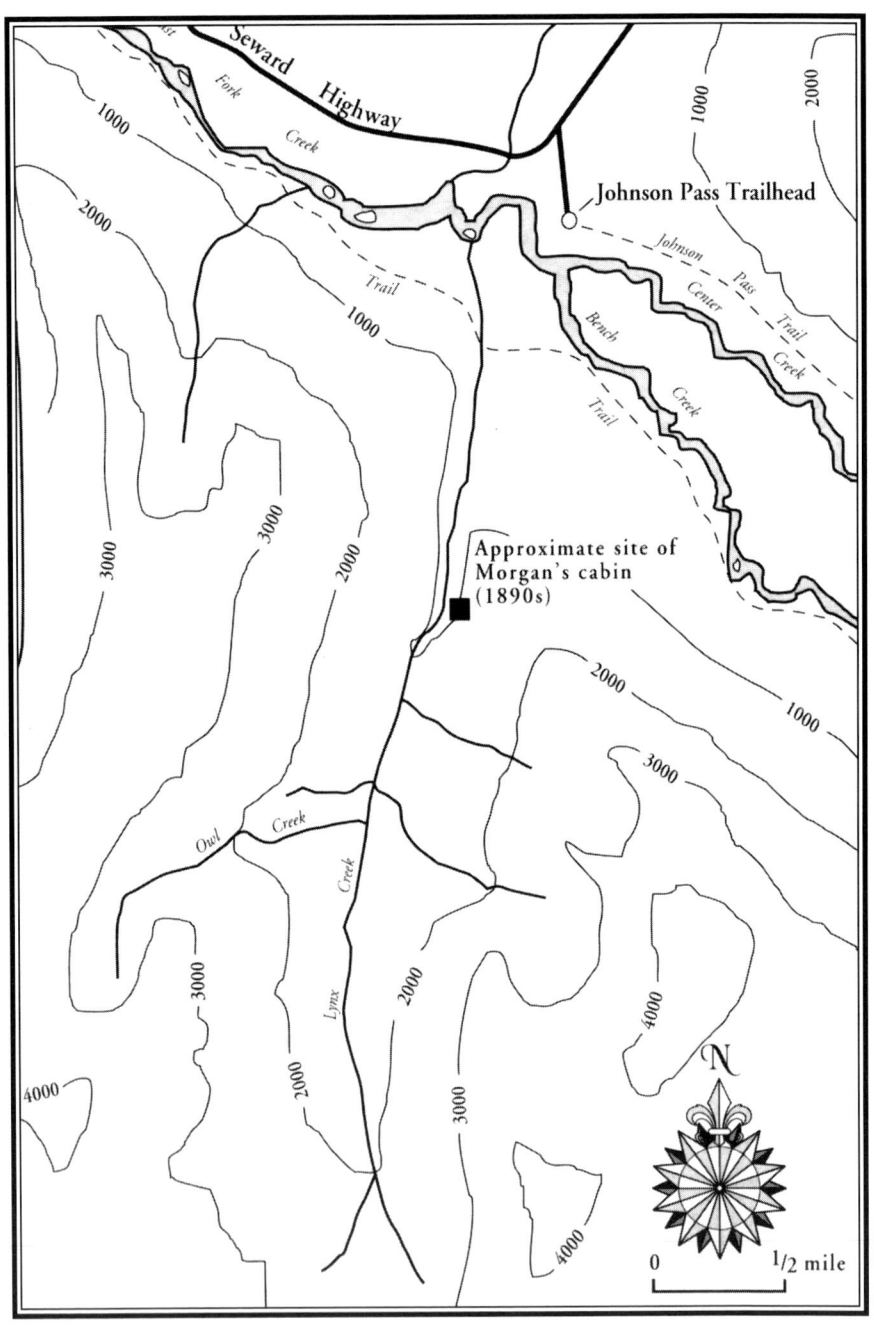

Map of Lynx Creek drainage, 1897, showing location of present-day
Seward Highway and Johnson Pass trail.

The fellow said: "You must have struck a rich paystreak."

"No," Phil said, "I just raised the price of my interest in the claim that much."

When Powers did not get back, Phil began to get worried. He complained that it would soon be freeze up time and here he was broke. They owed Wheeler's Store twelve hundred dollars and he did not know how much they owed the pack train. Besides, Bush and the other men had not been paid a cent out of the cleanup. Phil was afraid that Powers, instead of buying supplies, would get into a poker game and lose all the money, or spend it for whiskey. He said he just could not stand a winter in there broke. Finally, he asked me: "Have you got five hundred dollars with you?"

I said: "Well, I have got a draft on San Francisco for that amount and it will be cash when I sign it."

"Well," he said, "if you will give it to me, I will deed you my third interest in this claim."

Phil had brought up a hundred and fifty dollars with him so as to have money to get back on, but when they got to Sunrise Powers insisted on borrowing it so as to get started to work, and it was gone. "Powers should deed me a sixth interest so as to give me an even break with him."

"Well," I said, "it looks like I'm buying a big debt, but I think it will work out. If Bill Powers will agree to it, and agree to what we would do from then on, clean up together and start paying the debts off with the cleanup, I will do it."

Phil did not even go up to the cabin to get his hat. He shouted: "Here I go for Sunrise and we will be back tomorrow, or one of us will never come back."

Bush heard the conversation and said: "Jack, you have made a good deal."

Phil and Powers got back next day before noon, both walking fast and Phil was excited. Powers motioned for me to come out of the pit, and said: "Phil says you want to buy a half interest in the mine."

I said: "Yes, under the proper conditions, and I will tell you what they are now, and I don't want you to get offended if they do not suit you. In the first place, Phil says you have been taking cleanup to town to order stuff and pay for it. But you gamble it away and there is about a twelve hundred dollar store bill against the mine and a packing bill and that all these men here have not been paid. Is that true?"

He said: "Yes, that is right."

"Well," I said, "I will not stand for that a minute, and what I will propose is simply a business proposition; that is, that if I buy, we will clean up tonight. The pack train will be up tomorrow, and we'll pay the packer first and send [W. H.] Wheeler the rest. We'll clean up together right along and pay everything off as fast as possible, then after that divide the cleanup, each taking half."

"Shoveling in" on a creek near Sunrise, 1898.
PHOTO COURTESY OF DONALD CLICKNER, TROY, NEW YORK.

He studied a minute and said, "I don't see how anyone could object to doing business that way.

"I'm in favor of it, and I think it will be a good thing for me."

So I said that if it was satisfactory to him we would go up to the cabin. They could deed me a half interest in the mine and I would endorse the draft and give it to Phil. It did not take long, and Phil was so happy that he would not stay for lunch. He grabbed his things, stuck his draft in his pocket and away he went. I never saw him or heard from him afterwards, but I was glad that I was able to make him happy so he could get back to their saloon.

We were in good pay and the cleanup was more than I expected. We paid the packer out of it the next day, and sent the rest down to Wheeler. Powers felt so good that he told the packer to tell Wheeler to figure up all we owed him and send his bill up the next time the packer came, as we might have enough by that time to pay him in full. We did, and had some left.

When we were cleaning bedrock and the coarse gold showed up good, he would look at me and say: "Well, you are a lucky guy."

And I would say: "Yes, it looks that way now, but you're just as lucky, as the claim is practically clear now, and we will both have something left to carry us over the winter, if it holds up that good."

He would say, "Yes, that's right," and go to work again.

The last cleanup Powers kind of hesitated about paying the men. He said he would have to get his book and figure up what they had coming.

Bush and I moved into the cabin when Phil left and took his bunk. I told Powers that Bush was so good a worker, could do more than both the other men, that we should board him and pay him the usual wages. He agreed that it was all right. So we had been living like a family. Bush helped cook and wash dishes, and I thought things could not be much better. But one morning when Bush and I got up, Powers' bed was empty. I looked out and saw him walking up and down in the yard with a look on his face that I had never seen before. I did not say anything, but I did not like that look on his face. We got breakfast, and Bush went to the door and said: "Breakfast is ready, Billy, come on in."

Billy said he did not want any, and turned around and kept up his walking. I knew there was something wrong, but could not imagine what it was. We washed the dishes and I put on my hat and went to the door to go to work.

Billy came running toward me and said: "Morgan, pay Bush off. I don't want him here any longer."

I said: "What's the matter? Bush is the best man we can ever find."

He said: "Pay him off. I have been doped."[1]

I looked at him and asked: "My God, what's the matter with you? No one could dope you, and why should they?"

Bush said: "Pay me off, Jack. I can't stay here after that."

I was shocked so I could not talk. But I got the book and figured up what we owed him, and got the sack and weighed his gold.

Bush had got his things ready to go and came over and took me by the hand and said: "I hate to leave you here, as Billy is crazy, and you must keep your eye on him. If he makes a break toward you, brain him with a pick. Don't take any chances."

---

1   Drugged.

Just then the other two men came to the door and said they wanted their money, as they were afraid to stay there longer. We figured up what they had coming and I weighed out their gold. I set the sack back on the shelf where we kept it, and went out in the yard.

Billy said: "What are you going to do?"

I said: "I'm going to work, what else can I do?"

And he said: "Aren't you going to leave?

I replied: "Of course not. Everything I have got now is tied up in this mine. I am going to stay here and work it out, and you must come with me and help, as I am not leaving. I have never run away from anything yet, and am not going to start now. I own half of everything here, and got it at your suggestion. I am here to stay. Now, what are you going to do? You ought to know that no one could dope you, and why should they? You are the last man in the world I would want to dope, as I need you to help me work the mine. So go in and get your breakfast, and come on and help me."

He looked at me and said: "Maybe you are right. Go on, and I will be down there soon."

I turned the water in and started shoveling, and soon he came down and went to work. I noticed that the wild look had left his face.

Soon he said: "Maybe we should get [Lyman R.] Gale to help us, as he has worked all summer down on his claim and not made enough to keep him this winter, and no doubt will be glad to make a few dollars now."

I said: "Sure, go down and get him."

Gale came back with him smiling, and I could see that the boys had told him what had happened. We worked until near noon, when I told Billy he must do the cooking now so he could not think anyone could dope him. I told him to go up and get lunch ready and call us.

He said: "All right," and soon came out and called us.

That afternoon, about quitting time, another man came up and said he was looking for a job. I asked him if he could do that kind of work, and he said that was the only kind of work he ever did.

I asked Billy: "We can use him here, can't we?"

He said: "Sure, come on up to the cabin and get ready for dinner."

I felt mighty good about this fellow coming, as I was not sure that Billy was over his spell.

CHAPTER 5

WINDING UP THE FIRST SEASON

The four of us worked there until it froze up the 25th of September [1897]. Billy and I paid the other two off and cleaned up the boxes. I was going to pile them up when Billy said we would leave them, as it might soften up so that we could sluice some more. He said he was going to stay up there all winter, and not go to town at all. He ordered enough groceries to last him all winter. The pack train would be up again, maybe more than once, to take the people working above us down and bring up stuff for those who were going to stay.

We divided the gold, but he asked me if I wanted to pay half of the groceries, as he would be taking care of things there and doing some dead work during the winter. I said I'd be glad to. I got a lot of wood for him and piled it up in the woodshed in front of the house.

By that time I had met Fred Smith who had the adjoining claim above. He had crowded it and worked out his claim, which was much better than ours. Earlier he and Powers had gone up there together [in 1896] and had taken the two adjoining claims. Powers took one of his spells the first year they were there, and Smith gave him his choice. Powers took the lower claim ["J. R. No. 2"], as the channel was wider on it, and he thought it looked easier to work. But it seemed that most of the nuggets settled on Smith's claim ["J. R. No. 1"], which was good the whole length and not so deep to bedrock.

I went up to Fred Smith's camp after it froze up, and he was very friendly and invited me into his tent to show me his summer's cleanup. He pulled a gold pan out from under his bed and asked me if I could lift it. I could, but it was heavy, and I was sure there was over a hundred pounds of it. He said he thought there was about forty thousand dollars in it, and that he had more in Wheeler's safe, his cleanup for the year before. Smith said he had his claim worked out, but had bought the claim below us. However, he was going out to California that winter to spend some of it.

This Mr. White that I referred to earlier as looking for a job had got a job with Smith for himself, and for Mrs. White as cook for Smith's crew. He had a big cook tent and boarded his men.

The pack train took them to Sunrise, and Smith hired White to stay up there and take care of things that winter. Mrs. White went out on the boat that Smith went on, and I will have more to tell about this later on.

While I stayed on at Lynx Creek with Billy Powers, he was very pleasant and told me a lot about his past. There was one incident that amused me. When he built the cabin he had no windows in it, and left a place open in the roof about four feet square right over his table. He tacked an oiled cloth over it, as it would let in considerable light.

Sunrise, Alaska, 1896.
PHOTOGRAPH COURTESY OF *ALASKA SPORTSMAN.*

One night, the first winter he was there, he was sitting at his table re ading by candle light. The snow had piled up on the upper side of the cabin almost to the eaves. [Al] McEllaney, who had a claim farther up the creek had a female husky called Topsy who prowled around nights. This night when she came down she happened to walk on his roof and stepped on the oiled cloth skylight. It split with her weight and she and considerable snow came down onto his table and put out his light.

She started tearing around the cabin in the dark, turned over his stove, but there happened to be not enough fire in it to set the place afire. He said he did not know which was scared worse, he or Topsy. He finally found a match and lit his candle, saw it was Topsy and spoke to her, but she was so scared she kept running around. He opened the door and she went out of it like a black streak and never came back there again. He happened to have a piece of the oiled cloth left and tacked the new one on next day. It was still there, but after we moved in I boarded the hole up and we put two windows in the cabin.

I told Billy that I would likely get married by spring and bring my girl back with me. He said I should, as I was nearly thirty years old then. He said he'd had a chance to marry a good girl when he was about my age, but did not have the courage to do it. And he had regretted it ever since. He had lived a rough life and spent his money drinking and gambling, and said to look at him now and see what a wreck he was.

When I got all the wood that would go in the woodshed for Powers, I went to Sunrise and found that the last boat until October had gone out. Lathrop was there, and I asked him when he would leave to meet the *Dora* at Seldovia on her last trip out. He said that if I wanted to go back to the mine, if it softened up so we could sluice a few days, he would send a man up after me if it developed that he might want to go earlier.

I found our old friend Johnny Wood there when I got to Sunrise. He said that he and his partner did not make much on Bear Creek, as the channel had been worked out. But they had kept at it, thinking they might run onto a crevice in the bedrock that the miners had missed. He had run onto Dunton down at Hope, who with his partners had taken out some gold on Bird Creek. He got Wood to go over and stake a claim. Poor old Johnny thought he had a fortune in it. He had come back this year, 1897, and put in the summer over there, but found it would not pay to work. There was a little schooner in Sunrise then which was leaving for Seattle, in a few days. Wood was a good sailor, did not get seasick, and he went on the schooner. They had good winds, and he got back to Willapa long before I did.

While loafing there at Sunrise, we heard a bell ringing, and the man I was talking to said that it was calling a miners' meeting which we should go to. The meeting place was a large cabin almost filled up with men. Sam Mills was there. He was always chairman at the miners' meetings. He soon called the house to order and said a very serious matter had come up. A man had moved into Mr. Wood's house while he was away working his Canyon Creek claim. The man had used up the stuff Wood had left and had also carried all kinds of things from other cabins and filled the woodshed and house nearly full. Wood had fired him out, and got people who had lost stuff to come and get it. This man, no one knew his name, had moved into another vacant cabin. Mills appointed a couple of husky fellows to go and get him and bring him in.

When he came, I saw he was a big, tall man who had come on the boat with us from Seattle. He apparently worked his way on all the boats, as we would see him scrubbing around and helping. He was a German, I believe, and the boys called him Bismark. I think Mills appointed someone as prosecutor who asked Bismark if he moved into Mr. Wood's house and used his groceries, etc. Bismark said he found the door unlocked and stuff in there that no one was using. Then he was asked if he went into other houses and stole such food as he found there.

Bismark replied: "I no steal, just took the stuff that no one was using."

Then he was asked if he took such and such tools and stuff from different woodsheds. He said he found them, they were rusting, and he took them to Wood's place and took care of them. Then he was asked if he went into a cabin up at Boston Bar and stole some flour and stuff from the cabin and used it. He said he found it there, the mice were nibbling it, and he thought he had just as well use it.

William Tingley, who had been nicknamed "Windy Bill," had taken a claim at Boston Bar, where anyone could sluice up about a dollar a day by working when there was nothing else to do. He had built a cabin there and lived there most of the time. But that spring he had gotten a job with the Polly Mining Company and worked until it froze up that fall. Then he came down with the other men. He did not stop at his cabin, but came on to Sunrise, as he knew there would be a lot of free drinks when everyone got paid off. He stayed at Sunrise until then. He had sat very quietly until Bismark said he took the stuff from a cabin at Boston Bar. Then he raised up and asked: "Whose cabin was that?"

Wood said: "It was your cabin, Windy."

Windy jumped up and yelled: "Get a rope, boys, get a rope and we'll hang the s.o.b.!"

Mills said: "Order, Mr. Tingley, order."

Windy responded: "Order by g_d d___d, get a rope!"

When the Sunrise district was organized [in July of 1895], the miners passed a by-law or resolution that if anyone was caught stealing anything he would be hanged. And this had no doubt restrained anyone who had any inclination to take other peoples' stuff up to this time. No one locked their doors. Windy wanted to comply with the law, but someone got up and said he did not believe this man was all there. He did not think it would be right to hang a man of that kind, and he would make a motion to have him sent out of the district at once. Windy jumped up and said he would amend that motion, so that if he ever returned, the first man to put a bullet through him would get a reward of fifty dollars, and that he would be the one that would get it.

William "Windy" Tingley, with his Stevens New Model Pocket Rifle No. 40.
PHOTOGRAPH COURTESY OF THE GIRDWOOD HISTORICAL SOCIETY.

Mills appointed three men to take Bismark to the district line five miles down the Arm on the Hope trail. Windy was one of them, and Angus Kennedy, and a Mr. [William H.] Cook were the other two. Bismark refused to go, but Kennedy was a big husky, and he took him by the arms and boosted him in the seat a couple of times with his knee and he went along. They let him go by the cabin he was occupying then to get his things in a flour sack and take them with him. I went out and watched them go out of sight. There came up a snow squall that obscured them. They said Bismark refused to go on down the trail, but they told him that Windy had a rifle and would shoot him and get fifty dollars reward, if he came back across the line. They said that Windy gave him a couple of swift kicks in the stern to start him, and he kept going.

S. S. Dora.

It turned some warmer about the time Bismark was run out of town, and I went back up to the claim. Billy and I sluiced a few hours each day, and would clean up before the bottom of the boxes began to freeze. We got a few hundred dollars more to divide.

Loua [Louis H.] Lauriteson came up to tell me that I had better get down there by the 15th, as the boat might go out on the tide that day. I left Loua there with Billy. I suppose they took out some more gold by sluicing, as it kept mild for a couple of days longer.

When I went out on the *Perry* the 16th of October, 1897, it ran in to Hope on high tide to get the mail, and Bismark came aboard. I guess that Lathrop thought he could pay his fare, but no doubt would have let him go anyway, as the captains of all the boats seemed to cooperate in getting broke men back to Seattle. I noticed that Bismark was on both the other boats that I went down on, and I saw him scrubbing deck and rousting about. Captain [Edward] Kelly was the skipper.

It started snowing as we got out in the channel, and we could not see ten feet ahead. We ran over to Tyonek and anchored. The snow let up so we could see next morning, and Lathrop went over to the company store to get the last mail to go out. Mrs. [Tom W.] Hanmore came back with him on her way out, and she did not go back up there again.

The wind was coming up the Inlet, and it started to snow again. The *Perry*, which did not have much power, could not make much headway against the wind, and none against the wind and tide too. So we would anchor and wait for the tide to turn. And the waves would rock the little boat until I was seasick most of the time. There was a streak of coal along the south side of the Inlet, and they would anchor the boat as near as they dared to the bank. Lathrop's father and he and I would go ashore and pry out chunks of coal and put them in the dory and take a load to the *Perry*. We would throw the coal up on deck where John [O'Neil], the engineer, and Bismark would put it in the hold, until we finally filled the hold full. That was the only fuel they used while on the Inlet. The wind finally eased up and we got down to Seldovia and anchored in the little harbor.

The *Dora*, the boat we were to go out on, had not arrived there yet. And we were glad that she had stormy weather too, as we would have been late if she had been on time.

There was a coal mine operating on the east end of Kachemak Bay and a sailing schooner had loaded with coal there and came down to anchor near the *Perry*. The captain came over to get the news from up the Inlet. He and Captain Kelly were old friends. Kelly and his wife had planned to go on the *Dora* when she arrived, but the schooner captain told them he would like to have them go on his boat, as he could use Kelly's help. It was agreeable with Lathrop for them to go. I learned by the papers later on that Captain Kelly got a job on the steamer *Clara Nevada* as pilot running between Seattle and Skagway, and that the boat blew up coming down Lynn Canal [on February 5, 1898]. Everyone on board went down with her. So Captain is asleep in the deep with the others. It was sad, as he was a fine man as well as an able sea captain.

The steamer *Dora* was owned by the Alaska Commercial Company. It connected with their other boat at Kodiak and carried mail and passengers on the westward run to Dutch Harbor and back during the summer months. This was the *Dora's* last trip, and she went on to Juneau. She was loaded with passengers, and when we got on her we were crowded into the steerage. We took another boat at Juneau to get to Seattle.

CHAPTER 6

THE SECOND SEASON AT LYNX CREEK

When I got back to Willapa, I found that things had picked up. Jake Siler was building a little sawmill to saw spruce box lumber for a company in California, and he wanted some big boom sticks and piling. Bush and I got some timber on low tideland and put them in by hand. Bush was a superman and could lift almost as much as a steam donkey. I sold the cull logs that I had put in a slough for more than I got for the good logs before I left for Alaska. Bush and I cut some more logs, had them hauled, and kept busy most of the winter.

There was so much gold coming from Alaska that Fred Albright, part-owner in the large general store in South Bend, got the fever and wanted to buy a quarter interest in my claim, so I sold half my interest. I thought it would be a good idea to have a friend that I knew with me up there so that if Billy took one of his spells the two of us could no doubt handle him. And besides, I needed more money then as I was going to marry Lovicia Stratton and take her back with me.

We got married the 11th day of April, 1898, and went to Seattle on the train that day. There were several boats leaving for Cook Inlet, but the only one that we could get a stateroom on would not sail for a week. Albright went the day we did, and we had to wait a week in Seattle. It was lovely weather there in Seattle during that week, and we enjoyed it, as it was about the only honeymoon we had.

We bought a lot of groceries there, as Albright could get them at wholesale, and had them shipped on the boat we went on. They had worked this boat over and put in a number of staterooms on the lower deck. Albright got one of these. When we went across Dixon's Entrance the waves ran high on the side his room was on, and wet everything along that side. Albright sent a man up to tell me he was sick, and when I went down I found him breathing hard and all broke out with measles. We took him up and put him in our top bunk where it was dry and warm. There happened to be a young doctor on the boat who stayed right with Albright that day and night. He talked to him and told him to fight and fight to keep breathing. I think he had a touch of pneumonia, but he fought it off and his temperature went down some the next day. We did everything we could for him, and that doctor put in most of his time in the room. He [Albright] was some better when the boat got to Sunrise, and I carried him on my back up to the hotel about a half mile and got a room for him.

The L. J. Perry *docked at Hope, 1898.*
JOHN BROOKS COLLECTION, UNIVERSITY OF ALASKA FAIRBANKS.

Creason was going to leave soon so I bought a cabin from him. I arranged to get our things off the boat so we could be comfortable there. The captain anchored as near as he could to the wharf, and when the tide went out he started unloading the freight on the sand. Lathrop was there with the *Perry*. He could [reload and] unload it on the wharf when the tide got back in so he could get up to the wharf. "Copper River" was also there with his big mouth and wheelbarrow. He said he would take our freight up to the cabin for one dollar, and he got the job.

There was still a couple of feet of snow on the ground where there was no trail. The trail was open to The Forks, as the pack train had been over it, but the snow was melting on the side and water was running into the trail. There was an old maid named Shepard who came on the boat with us. She was glad to stay with my wife until the trail was opened all the way so she could go up with the pack train and ride one of the horses.

I walked up to The Forks, and it was awful. The slush was about knee deep along most of the way. I stayed all night there, as the trail had not been broken from there on. It was too late for a crust on the snow, and it was impossible to follow the trail as one would go into the snow about two feet or more. I thought I could make it by following the creek, and I did. I would work along one side of the creek until I ran against a bluff. I waded back and forth until I got to Lynx Creek and made it to the claim before dark.

Powers seemed kind of grumpy. He said I ought to have been there two weeks earlier, as we could have been sluicing.

"Well," I said, "let's go out to the cut and see if we can sluice now."

The water had run down into the cut and frozen it full of solid ice.

I said: "It don't look much like sluicing now, does it, but let's turn enough water over it to melt in a few days."

Then I said: "Did you and Loua saw out enough boards to floor the cabin, as you planned to when I left?"

He said: "No, I decided to go to Sunrise soon after you left. I stayed down there all winter and just got back a week or so ago."

"Well," I said, "let's get the whipsaw out and see if we can saw enough boards to cover the floor while that ice is thawing out of the cut."

He agreed. We made enough boards to floor the cabin by the time the ice got out. Everything worked so much better than he expected that he got quite cheerful, and when the ice was out we set up the boxes and went to shoveling. We found the pay still good, and cleaned up every night for the first two days. The third day we ran on to a hard streak of bedrock with nothing on it and not much in the gravel. Billy stood and looked at it.

"Do you suppose the Russians worked good spots along this side?" he asked.

"No, we could find their rock piles if they had. The pay streak runs around this hard streak, and we will soon get over it."

The next morning when I got up I saw him outside walking back and forth with that wild look on his face.

I got breakfast and opened the door and said: "Come in, Billy, breakfast is ready."

I knew what he would say, so I went in, ate my breakfast, got ready, and started out to go to work.

He asked: "Where are you going?"

"Down in the cut to work," I said. "Go in and get your breakfast and come on down."

He said: "No, I am doped again."

"Well," I said, "what did you dope yourself with and what for? You ought to know better than that by this time."

He said he was going to town, and got his coat and hat, and struck out down the trail in a swift walk. I watched him go out of sight. He never looked back once.

Miners using hand mining methods on a creek in the Sixmile drainage, 1898.
Photograph courtesy of Donald Clickner, Troy, New York.

Most of the groceries we bought for him to winter on were still there, and I had plenty to eat. I went to work and soon got over that hard bedrock and into pay again. A few days later on the pack train came up and brought some of our groceries from the cabin. The packer said he told my wife she had better not start then as he was not sure he could get all the way through. He brought a letter from Wheeler that stated he had bought Powers' half interest in the mine and was sending a couple of men up to help me. They were both good men, George Perkins and [Angus] McDonald. I don't believe I ever knew his first name, as we called him Mac. Both these men worked for me all the way through, and I think they liked me as much as I did them.

My wife came up on the next trip of the packtrain and we had a time cleaning up the cabin. She worked hard and seemed to enjoy it. She was an excellent cook, and soon got used to the little Yukon stove. She baked good bread. McDonald boarded with us. Perkins brought a tent and stove and batched.

Wheeler also came up with her that trip, and I showed him what we were doing and that we were on good pay. I got the sack down and gave him half the gold. He took Perkins out and talked to him awhile. Then he came to me and said several of the old miners in Sunrise wanted him to let them run the mine. But he was satisfied with the way I was running it and said to keep it up the same way. He sent up another man, and Albright also came up later, but could not do much yet. I put him on the payroll. He watched around and would go up in the timber to get poles and bring them down, as we had to have a couple of poles every box length.

We had been at work about two weeks this spring of 1898 when a man named Clark came up and introduced himself as a mining engineer from San Francisco. He said he supposed I knew Fred Smith and Mrs. White. I said I met them there at Fred's camp the fall before, but did not know much about them.

Clark said they went to the St. Francis Hotel in San Francisco, and Fred kept sober. When he sold his gold he kept out a bunch of nuggets and had them in each of his pants pockets. When the mining men who stayed at the hotel would get together and discuss the reports of the gold that was coming from Alaska, Fred would horn in and say he just came from there, that he had a mine and brought out some gold and was spending it. He told them he was going back in the spring to get more. They asked him if the gold was coarse or fine, and he said both, as there were nuggets on the bedrock and fine gold in the gravel. He ran his hand into his pocket and pulled out a handful of nuggets, and when they had looked them over he put them back in his pocket and stuck his hand into the other pocket and pulled out another handful and said that was what the nuggets looked like. He said that really excited all of them, and they asked Fred all about where his mine was, and how much ground he had. He showed them a crude map he had made showing what he said were his claims. He had bought the claim below ours, and had located claims on the bench alongside of his claims and ours, which made a nice layout for a mine. They asked him if he would sell his mine, and he said no, he would not sell it, but might sell a half interest in it to good mining people who could run it. He wanted a half million dollars for a half interest, but would accept fifty thousand down and balance as five percent of the cleanup each year until it was paid. If the mining company would buy, he insisted, they would have to take a real outfit of pipe, lumber, tools, etc., to run a big hydraulic mine. And if they did not operate it so it would pay, everything, including ground and all equipment, would revert to him.

Clark said this looked like a fair proposition, and that Fred Smith seemed to be a good, honest, old fellow. So he and some others went in on it. He said they brought a boat load of stuff, the captain was anxious to get started back, and he unloaded it before Clark found out that they had been taken in by old Fred. Clark said that if he had known the situation, he would have sent it all back. However, he said he could sell some of the stuff, especially the groceries.

He said that he understood that Smith and Mrs. White came in early, before the Arm opened up so that boats could get in. They landed at Seward and got Indians to sled them and their money and lots of whiskey over to Sunrise. There he had bought one of the saloons and the hotel and had set up a bar in each, and was drinking a lot of the booze himself. Clark said that when he asked Fred to go with him and show him the mine, the old fellow had to hang onto the bar rail to stand up. He said he could not go, but that Morgan was up there working a claim adjoining their mine and would be glad to show him the ground and the lines.

I told Clark when he showed me Fred's map that he had our claim marked as his. He said he found this out on the record down at Sam Mills' office. I went with him to Smith's upper claim, and showed him how it all lay, and the line between Smith's claim and ours. He said anyone could see it's no hydraulic proposition. He asked me if there was any place his men might make wages shoveling, as he had brought up some good workers and would like to get work for them for the summer. He had lots of tents and tools, and perhaps groceries enough to feed quite a crew all summer.

I told him that [John L.] Jerry O'Dale and old man Gale ran a cut at the lower end of the claim below us. They got to bedrock before it froze up, and they said it paid a little better than wages when they quit. I went down with Clark and showed him the layout, and he said he would have the pack train bring up a half dozen tents, and tools and cooking outfit for a small crew and put them to work.

When they got to work and cleaned up Clark found it paid better than wages. He hired as many men as he could work, and worked out the best of the pay dirt by the time it froze up. He stayed right with the crew and kept them busy, worked two shifts. When it froze up he came up to say goodbye. He said he was not going to take the boxes down, as old Fred would fall heir to them. Clark could not sell the tools or tents, as the country was flooded with that kind of stuff. Many people came in that spring thinking they could find gold anywhere, and went off and left such stuff as they could not sell it. Clark said he guessed it served them right to let an old s.o.b. like Fred Smith get them in such a mess. He said he could not even give him a good licking, as the old drunk could not even hold up his hands to protect himself. Clark left on the first boat out, and I never heard from him again.

Fred and Mrs. White got married, and he sobered up after Clark left. He seemed to be a decent old cuss, good to get along with. Of course, he fell heir to a lot of lumber and pipe, and got his ground back, but never made the mine pay again. He leased some of it to others and got a percentage. He was so agreeable and nice to me that I could not help liking the old cuss.

Miners preparing to depart Sunrise for the trail up the Sixmile.
JOHN BROOKS COLLECTION, UNIVERSITY OF ALASKA FAIRBANKS.

When I first came up the creek this spring I ran into [Frank H.] Waskey and [James] Wallace. They had come in on an early boat and gone up to The Forks where they bought a fraction of a claim three hundred feet long on the East Fork just below the mouth of Gulch Creek. They wanted to know who I was and where I was going, etc.

When I told them, they said: "Oh, yes, you have interest in a good claim on Lynx Creek."

I asked them how they were going to work the ground. They said they would pump the water out, and run the gravel through a rocker, as they were sure that all the creeks were lousy with gold on the bedrock. I told them that I knew they were not, as I had gone to bedrock on most of them last year when prospecting. That seemed to disturb Waskey, and he asked me if I would give him a job in the fall so he could have a grubstake if they did not strike it. I told him I would if I happened to need a man.

Waskey came up a few days before the freeze up and we gave him a few day's work. It happened that it froze hard enough so we had to quit sluicing the 25th of September every year I was there. There were a couple of fellows we knew at South Bend who had come up with the Bird Creek bunch and worked over there until they found out that they could not make much. They came up, and we gave them work enough to earn money to get back home. Everything worked along good till we had to quit.

Albright was satisfied and so was Wheeler. Before Albright left, we went down to the cut, and he said that he surely liked the way I ran the thing, as I was on the job every minute, never let the boxes fall down, or the rock pile tumble, or the drain ditch fill up, and never let the water slop over the wing dam and fill the drain ditch. He said the ground was not as rich as we thought it might be, but he knew we got all of it. He went down to Sunrise and went out on the first boat.

I think that Perkins stayed and helped me take the boxes down before he left. It was nice weather, but cold enough to freeze ice in the boxes.

Mrs. Morgan and I stayed up at Lynx Creek awhile and ceiled the cabin overhead. We killed some grouse and ptarmigan, then went down to Sunrise and fixed up our cabin there so we could be comfortable through the winter.

We found that [William L.] Jack and Nellie Frost had a cabin next to ours and Hugh Anderson and his family on the other side. They were all fine people. We had wondered how we would be accepted in the community, and soon found that everyone was friendly and sociable. As I remember now, there were about a dozen men with their wives there and possibly fifty or sixty bachelors. C. [Cyrus] F. Yeaton, a fine man, was in charge of the U.S. Mercantile Company store. H. [Harry] A. Smith had taken over the Alaska Commercial store when Al Creason left, and Mr. Wallace took charge of Wheeler's store for the winter. Wheeler always went out for the winters.

There were two saloons. A man named [W. H.] Orr ran one of them, and Scotty Watson the other. They had big log houses and kept the places warm so the boys could loaf and play cards there late. Neither of them made much money, as the camp was not rich enough. Soon after we got there someone proposed that we build a hall for entertainment. There had been some lumber shipped up there that was not the grade ordered, and it was for sale cheap. They passed the hat and got enough money to pay for it. There was a good carpenter there, named [William H.] Cook, who took charge and planned the building. The lumber was not what was required, but he marked it out and a number of us whipsawed it into the proper dimensions.

Everyone got in and helped where they could, and we soon had a nice hall. The main floor was big enough for dancing and there was a stage in one end where they put on plays for entertainment. We got in wood enough to keep it warm all the time, if someone wanted to use it. There was some kind of an entertainment every Saturday night, and after the play was over those who

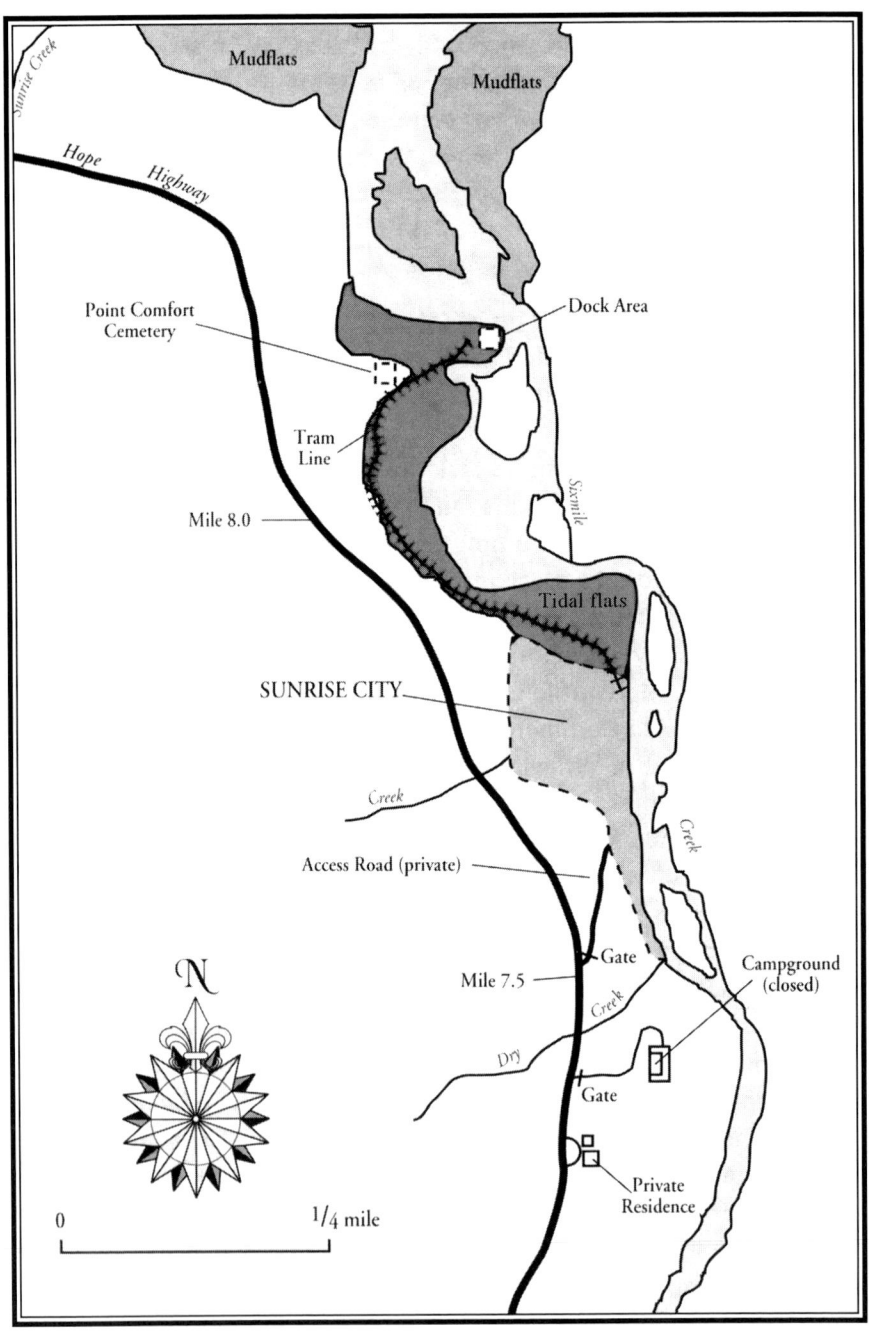

Map of Sunrise, Alaska, 1898, showing location of present-day Hope Highway.

could dance danced until one or two o'clock. A fine young man named Frank Ahlburg had a good violin and was always ready to play gratis when he was needed. There were several who could sing, and all were willing to do anything they could to help.

There were a few romances too. A Miss Shepard, who was on the boat we came in on, married a man with a long red beard. He was not gray, but she was as white as a sheep, and I imagine much older than he was. He had a cabin at Hope, and they lived there. But they came to Sunrise to dances and entertainments. She seemed very happy. The second winter during an entertainment at Hope, just after the midnight dinner, he dropped dead. She was heartbroken and thought someone poisoned him. I suppose his heart stopped. Anyway, she went back to Michigan in sorrow, but had the satisfaction of having had her romance. I think she had money, as they both dressed well, and they said he did not work after they got married.

A widow came up there and married [M. L.] Harry Gleason. Gleason had a claim well up on Lynx Creek, and it was still paying to work it then. She had a grown son who was an epileptic, and he worked for Harry. Harry Hosin told me that he worked for Gleason one summer, and he and this boy were shoveling on each side of the sluice boxes. This boy told him that he sometimes had fits. And if he should have one there, throw some water in his face. He fell over one day and began to roll around, and Harry stuck his shovel in the water in the sluice box. He got it too deep and threw a big stream in the boy's face.

The boy jumped up swearing, and Harry said: "You told me to throw water in your face if you had a fit."

He said: "Yes, but I didn't tell you to drown me!"

The next year this boy was at Hope with three fellows who came in there. They started back to Sunrise in a boat and capsized. One of them drowned at once, but the other two and this boy got hold of the boat and hung on. It swung in near the shore just below Sunrise, and this boy jumped off and yelled to the others to come ashore, but they hung onto the boat. It swung back into the current and they were drowned. He [later] disappeared from Sunrise, but when we came out on the boat from Sunrise, it went into Seward to pick up passengers. The wind came up and was kicking up white caps. We saw a skiff with two men in it coming toward us and it upset near our boat. A couple of men jumped in a boat and picked them up. When they came on our boat, one of them was the epileptic boy.

Another young fellow was known as Colonel [Harry E.] Revelle. Everyone liked him, and one day someone asked if he was a real Colonel. Someone laughed and said no, that Revelle did belong to the Army for a while and was stationed near Tacoma under a Colonel who took an interest in him. The Colonel had him take care of his quarters. One night Revelle went into town with some of the other soldiers and thought it would be a good idea to wear the Colonel's uniform, as it fitted him. When they got to town, they had too many drinks. They got into a fight and all got locked up. The Colonel went in the next day and got them out, and being good natured, just had Revelle clean up his uniform. Revelle was forever the Colonel after that.

Jack Frost and his dogs, Sunrise, 1898.
PHOTOGRAPH COURTESY OF DONALD CLICKNER, TROY, NEW YORK.

Across the creek from our entertainment hall Scotty Watson had a still, and Frank Waskey ran it for him that winter. I don't suppose he ever saw a still before, but he was chock-full of energy and would tackle anything.

The camp had a big entertainment every Christmas, and the women made up a bag of candy and nuts for everyone with his name on it. Waskey played Santa. He came over from the still and put on the Santa suit. He would pull a bag out of the box and read the name and say something to rhyme with the name, like "Jack Morgan plays the organ." When he came to Scotty Watson's bag he read off: "Scotty Watson, with all your faults, we love your still." That brought the house down.

There was a young fellow from Boston named John [H.] Brownlow who could recite and read pathetic pieces so good that you could think you could see the thing as it happened. There was a young fellow named [Ethan A.] Thompson who was something of an actor. He had been with a troupe that played "Jekyll and Hyde" and he wrote the parts, picked a cast to play it, and worked with them until they all knew their parts. As I remember, some of it was not very good, but he played "Jekyll and Hyde" himself and did it so well the house cheered him for at least fifteen minutes.

This [next] amusing incident happened the first day of January, 1899. There was a claim on Canyon Creek whose owner did not come in to work his assessment the year before. Everyone knew that it would be vacant that first of January. There was a nice old couple named Anderson who came up there a few years before this and bought a house in Sunrise. He worked around the claims summers. Since there were two other Anderson families in Sunrise, someone called this man Potlatch Anderson.

Mrs. Anderson was ambitious, and like some others thought that all the claims on Canyon Creek were full of gold. They got up to this claim before midnight. And when she got down to the claim line, old Joe [Joseph] Wilson was there with a notice on a stake to set up at midnight. This particular claim was at the lower end of the long deep canyon, and the creek was already frozen over with two feet of settled snow on it then. The sled trail had been broken by that time, and there were two feet of solid snow on each side of the trail. Mrs. Anderson had tried to talk Wilson out of putting up his stake, telling him that they were an old couple and needed money to live on, and that he ought not take bread out of her mouth. But he said he was old and hungry, too, and was there first. She started to turn around and tripped against the snow bank on the side of the trail and fell over backwards on the snow. I have done it myself sometimes, and have seen others do it.

Old Joe said: "You might as well get up, as you can't buy me off with that. I'm too old and way past that stage."

She told the women about it and said: "The old heathen."

The women thought it was a good joke.

Alaska Commercial Company Store, Sunrise.
JOHN BROOKS COLLECTION, UNIVERSITY OF ALASKA FAIRBANKS.

They both staked their notices at midnight, and as I remember they met at the next miner's meeting July 4th. Each told his story, and the committee awarded each a half interest in the claim.

I don't know whether Joe and [Bob] McKay tried to work it that year or not, as I forgot to ask McKay about it. However, it had washed so deep that they could not get a wing dam[1] on it. It may be full of gold and it may not. I suppose

---

1   A technique of diverting water to one side of the creek, thereby enabling miners to work the stream gravels directly below the dammed portion of the creek.

now that with a diver's suit someone could go down and find out, if the current is not too swift for them.

Mrs. Anderson cooked for [Simon William] Wible the year I worked there. The old man was a good worker, too. I don't know how long they stayed up there. After Wible worked out his high bars [bench claims on lower Canyon Creek], they said that old Joe Wilson took some of his pipe and lumber across the creek onto a high bar on that side, ran a ditch from a little creek and set up and piped off the little bar. He cleaned up thirteen thousand dollars that fall. His strike lasted him only that winter.

When the river froze up around the first of January, 1899, the people who had claims that they worked bought all the heavy groceries like flour, sugar, rice, and canned goods and sledded them up to the claims. I bought a good sled and sledded up enough to last us through the coming season. We would take the stuff up to The Forks, pile it up in Rivers' big bunk house and go back to Sunrise to get a load for next day. When we got all we had up that far, we'd go up and sled it on up to our mines. We would stay at the mine cabin at Lynx Creek, and make a round trip each day. We would save ten cents a pound by sledding. As I remember now, there were twenty-five or thirty sleds in line as we left Sunrise. From The Forks on, some went to Mills Creek, some to Canyon Creek, and some to Lynx Creek. When we got the trail in good shape we could go right along with a couple of hundred pounds or more. Those who had a good dog could haul three or four hundred pounds.

There was a fellow who got his hands frozen that winter. He was taken to meet the boat and then to the nearest hospital, where they amputated one hand and left only a finger and thumb on the other.

Everyone cheerfully donated when anyone had to be sent out, even those who could ill afford to help. It seemed that it was really like one big family when anyone was in trouble.

Frank Ahlburg had another very narrow escape, but I don't believe he ever realized how near he came to the end this time. When all our supplies were sledded up the creek, Kingsley Smith said that he had found a nice quartz stringer up above Mills Creek the year he worked there. He suggested we go and shoot out some of it and test it, as he saw some free gold in a sample he had knocked off. So he and Frank and I went up to Mills Creek, as the weather was nice, though still cold. We took a sledge, drill, ax, and some dynamite. The trail over to the Sound was open and went within a quarter of a mile of the ledge, and that side of the trail was a mountain with nothing growing on it. We had to break steps up the bare mountain with the small ax, as there was a heavy crust on the snow then, and it was too steep to climb with snowshoes. We got up there and put in a shot and got pieces of the quartz to take with us.

Kingsley said we could sit down on the back end of our snowshoes and ride down the mountain side. Both he and I had noticed that there was an abrupt breakoff right straight below us that was almost a straight fall into a deep depression where young alders had grown up about six feet high and very close together. He said to steer off to the left and go around this. He had a sledge to steer with, I had the drill, and Frank had the ax. We watched Kingsley go down, and then I started and had no trouble steering around this jump-off. Then Kingsley yelled to Frank to come on, and waved at him to steer off to the left.

I really don't know what struck Frank to come straight down. Maybe he did not notice the jump-off. Anyway, he came straight down and we both yelled and waved at him to swing to the left. He came straight for the break, and did not try to slow up. He held the ax up in his hand, and was almost flying when he came over the hump. Apparently when he flipped over the hump he went over once, I know. But Kingsley said he turned over three times, as we would see a snowshoe, then the ax, then the white cap with a red tassel on top that Frank wore. He was going so fast that he did not strike the alders until almost the last of them, where they were the thickest and tallest, and he happened to strike them with his backside and his feet ahead of him. The alders bent down, but not to the ground. Of course, they sprang up some, and there he was sitting on the back of his snowshoes just as he was when he came down. His momentum had carried him out to the trail.

It was all over in seconds. I held my breath until he got to the trail. He was sitting up, still holding the ax as high as he could and let out a pitiful wail as loud as he could: "Ooooouuuuu." We ran to him and asked him if he was hurt, and he said: "Yes, I'm killed."

We got his feet out of his snowshoes and he got up, shook himself, felt of his legs and arms, and said: "Well, I guess I'm all here."

Then it occurred to us that it was funny. We were so glad he was not killed we had to laugh, and really that pitiful wail of his was funny when we realized he was not hurt much. One would naturally say that the Lord must have been with him, but we know that the Lord does not pay any attention to little things like that. His escape from his crazy friend was from his good judgment, but this time it was pure, bullheaded luck. For if he had hit the brush with his head, his momentum would have sent him right through the brush and into the frozen snow which would have broken his neck.

CHAPTER 8

MINING WITH "MAGE" AND "BOB"

The summer of 1899 I hired Lafe [Lafayette J.] Cline and Kingsley Smith, who had not been able to make wages on their claims and wanted a job for the next year. The Smiths had a little girl who was born at Sunrise in January, 1898, and they named her Addie Alaska. She was big enough to run around the yard when they moved up to the mine and put their tent up in our yard. The Clines also put up a tent in the yard, and there were two good women and the little girl to keep Mrs. Morgan from getting lonely that summer.

Frank Ahlburg and Smith were great chums, and Frank moved up and worked for us that summer. Of course, there was not much sociability as the season was so

Sunrise, Alaska, late 1890s.
U.S. FOREST SERVICE, ANCHORAGE.

short it crowded the work. We even worked Sundays, and the men were all very tired evenings. Perkins and I worked fast and hard, and the others thought they had to keep pace with us, and it was hard on them. I would not have complained if they had not worked so hard, but it all helped.

Frank Ahlburg had yet another very narrow escape while in Sunrise. A friend of his went haywire and decided that he had to kill Frank. Frank saw him coming toward his cabin with an ax, saying: "I have to kill you, Frank, but I will not hurt your violin."

Frank had noticed that this fellow had been acting strange, and closed his door and held it closed. The man ran against the door a couple of times and Frank held it. Then the fellow backed up and made a hard run at it. Frank jerked the door open and the fellow fell on the floor. Frank jumped on him, yelling for help. The man next door ran in, and I think they tied the man up and kept him until a boat was due at Prince William Sound. I don't remember who took him over to meet the boat. I think the government took charge of such patients then and sent them down to Portland to the Morningside Hospital.

At the end of the summer of 1899, Kingsley Smith sold a claim he had on Canyon Creek to Simon Wible, a real miner who came from [Bakersfield] California. Kingsley had decided to take his wife and daughter Addie Alaska away from that country. Mrs. Cline went out, too, and Mrs. Morgan went with them on the same boat that fall, as she did not want to stay there another winter without a doctor or dentist. Also, she had learned that her mother [Rebecca Stratton of Willapa] was not well, and she thought she ought to go out and help take care of her during the long winter.

I had decided that I would stay there until we could work the claim out. I thought by hard work and by being careful, we could save enough to go into a paying business when we left there. And it was expensive to go out and stay all winter. We also needed some new [sluice] boxes which I could make that winter as well as sled up the heavy groceries.

Kingsley Smith had a small dog named Mage, and a manx cat named Bob. He was going to leave them, and asked me if I would keep them. I was glad to get Mage, as I saw when we were sledding that he liked to help pull the sled, and would pull the whole load if he could. I had not paid much attention to him there at the mine, just noticed that he kept near little Addie Alaska, when she wandered around outside.

The Smiths were packing up getting ready to leave. Mage came over to our cabin, came in and put his head against my knee, and sat down beside me. It really looked like he had understood what they had said. The Smiths went on to Sunrise to get ready to go on a boat that was to leave soon. I went down with Mrs. Morgan a few days before the boat was to sail, helped her get ready to go, and saw them all leave on the boat. Mage stayed right by me all the time, and never went near the Smiths. He was a great companion. He seemed to understand everything I said to him, and was almost human. No, I will take that back, for there was not a mean, contemptible, selfish streak in him. He was just a good, kindhearted, faithful, loving dog, ready to do his part and more, too, when the opportunity offered.

Sam Mills' claim near The Forks, at the mouth of Canyon Creek, 1904.
F. H. MOFFIT #198, U. S. GEOLOGICAL SURVEY, DENVER, COLORADO.

I went back up to the mine that day and found Bob there waiting for me. I had sawed a little piece out of the bottom of the door and hung it so it would swing each way so Bob could shove it either way by pushing on it with his head. I had to show him only once how it worked and he seemed to like to go in and out that way. We left some food for him, and he made himself at home there. I had a lot of things to do, and Mage and Bob went with me everywhere I went, except when we went to Granite Creek to kill a mess of grouse for the table. Bob would climb the nearest tree and wait for us until we came back. He liked the heads and feet of the birds, but was crazy about the fish heads when we would go down to the East Fork and catch a mess of fish for a change.

It warmed up a few days after we got back up there, and I set up the boxes and sluiced a few hours for a few days. Both Bob and Mage were right at my heels all the time, and stayed and watched me clean up. Wheeler's man sent up a man to help me whipsaw lumber for [sluice] boxes and riffles, and Mage would go with us and watch us. We would build a fire for him to stay by, as it was getting cold then. He would lie there and watch us, and when there came enough snow, he was glad to help me sled to the mine. Nothing made him as happy as getting into his harness to help pull the sled. I don't believe I would have gotten lonely if they had not been there. I had plenty of reading matter, as a number of our friends sent us a box of their old magazines every summer. But I found that it was very interesting to study both dog and cat and learn how understanding animals can be.

It softened up a few days in October, so I could sluice a few hours while the sun shone. But I would have to clean up and turn the water out of the boxes as soon as the sun would go out of sight behind the mountain.

Bob went out with us the first morning that I turned the water into the boxes. He climbed into the boxes and was coming up toward me, but I did not see him until the water went roaring down the boxes. Instead of jumping out of the boxes, he ran back down. He was going so fast that when he came to a cleat across the box, he turned a somersault. But he got up and ran again with the water near his heels until he got to the end of the string and jumped out. Mage and I enjoyed the race hugely, and I whooped and yelled and Mage ran around in a circle barking.

The next morning Bob did it all over again. It occurred to me then that he had a streak of humor in him, and did it this time to entertain Mage and me.

There was snow enough just before Christmas to take the sled to Sunrise, and I decided to go down and take in the holiday entertainments there. So we put Bob in a box and tied it on the sled and took him with us. When we would go over to the stores evenings, Bob would go with us and would jump up on a wood pile and wait until we would come out to go home. Mage would go in the stores, as everyone liked him and made a lot of him.

The river froze over so we could sled by the first of January. I bought the heavy groceries and Mage and I sledded them up to The Forks. I had put a box up overhead in the woodshed for Bob to stay in. I just had to show him once how to climb up the ladder and he would stay there while we were gone. Our neighbor

[Hugh] Anderson said he saw a dog go into the woodshed and start barking up at Bob. Bob waited until the dog turned around, and jumped down on his back and stuck his claws into the dog.

The dog started howling and running back toward his home, and Bob rode him a ways, then jumped off and came back looking perfectly satisfied over the performance. Anderson said that the dog never came there again as long as Bob was there.

The last load to take up was a light one, so we put Bob in his box in the sled and started early. We went all the way to the mine that day. Then we went down to The Forks every morning and brought up a load until we got it all up to the cabin. Bob was satisfied to stay and keep house while we were away. It seemed that he understood that he could not go, and never offered to follow when we were sledding. But when we would go hunting he seemed to know where we were going, and would go a way with us and wait for us until we came back.

There were lots of mice up in that country, and they would come in and get under the house to keep warm. Bob would sneak out and catch them when they would come out in the woodshed where I had wood piled up on both sides of the gangway through the shed. A weasel also moved in under the floor where it was warm, and there he stayed. Bob resented his being there and often sneaked out to try to catch him, but the weasel was quick and would get back under the floor or in the wood. It got to be a regular game with them, and I think the weasel liked the fun.

But he got careless one night and Bob eased his way out of the door and caught him. There was an awful fight, with the weasel screeching and Bob yowling. Mage jumped against the door trying to get out to help Bob. I moved the lamp and set it down so it would throw the light out in the runway, and opened the door. The light, I think, made Bob lose his hold on the weasel, which dragged itself back under the floor. We never saw or heard it again, and I think it died there from the bites Bob gave it.

While sledding the stuff from The Forks, I would tie the shotgun on the sled. There were ptarmigan along the trail in places feeding on the young willows, and I nearly always got a few to take home as they were our principal meat that winter. One trip coming up, a marten ran across the trail and into the timber. I got the gun off the sled, followed his tracks in the timber, and met him coming back. He ran up a tree when he saw me, and stuck his head around to look at me and I shot him.

This was the first marten tracks I had seen, as some of the miners trapped them all out before I got there. These had come back from some parts that had not been trapped. Someone had left a bunch of traps at the cabin, so I brought one down the next day and followed the marten backtrack across the river on the ice. I set the trap at the foot of a spruce tree, baited it with a ptarmigan wing and found a nice marten in it the next morning. So when we got the groceries all sledded up I took some traps, and Mage and I went over in the Granite Creek timber and set them. We caught twenty marten that winter, a few mink, and one wolverine. It was all interesting, as I saw a lot of country and I learned something about the animals up there.

I have read several articles that trappers wrote about the wolverines being hard to catch. I set my traps on top of the snow and hung a bait up over them. Every marten that came along would dance around until he would get in the trap, and two wolverines also walked up to get the bait and stepped right in the traps. They twisted the chains off and went up to where there was a little ridge of broken up granite two to three hundred feet high and three miles long extending along between Granite Creek and the East Fork. They went into the rocks and I imagine died in there, as I never saw tracks of them with the traps. I found some heavy wire and tied it to a trap and caught one of the wolverines, as he could not break the wire. He, too, walked right into the naked trap like the others, but I was sorry I got him, as his skin was as hard to clean as a bear skin. I had to put in several nights scraping the fat off of it and drying it.

I found that the marten often went in pairs, and when one would get in a trap, the other one would hide under the nearest windfall and stay there until we came to the trap. Mage rousted the marten out and went after it, but the snow was not hard enough to hold Mage up. While the marten ran on top of it, Mage would go into the snow up to his belly. The marten would get ahead of Mage, then wait for him until he would get up near, having a regular circus with Mage. But finally it came in reach of the shotgun. I got two this way. It seemed that they were very curious, or had playful streaks and liked the racing. I went up on the mountains and saw a few fox tracks high up. They did not come near us, as they seemed to know that a man was dangerous. Maybe some of them had been caught in traps and got out.

I learned how the ptarmigan spent the nights. They would stay down in the flats and feed on the willows during the days. When it got dark they would fly up above the timber line, zip down in the snow, and make a nice hole to stay in, none of them very close together. This was to make it hard for the fox and wolverines to find them. I suppose that after the snow got a crust on which they could not break, they went into the old holes they had made.

A mink moved in and went under our floor after the weasel died. Bob did not want anything to do with him, but Mage was anxious to get at him. I got up one morning after daylight and Mage wanted out while I was dressing. He soon came back, went over to where the shotgun was hung in a rack and reared up under it. He barked, looked at me and ran out again. I thought he wanted me to get the gun and go out. I did, and when I got out I saw the mink going down toward the rock pile. It could go on the crust on the snow, but the snow would break through with Mage, who knew he could not catch it. No doubt he remembered about the marten and knew the gun was the medicine for it.

It was early spring, and there was only a foot and a half of snow on the ground when it settled. I had made the sluice boxes and riffles we would need, and turned the water in the cut to thaw the ice out. McDonald came up [from Sunrise] and we set up the boxes and started sluicing when the mornings would warm up so that the water would not freeze in the boxes.

Mrs. Morgan had come in on the first boat that got to Sunrise. She surprised us by coming up on the first pack train that came up to bring some of the fellows and their outfits to work on some of the Smith claims. Mage and Bob both remembered her and Mage went around in circles barking with joy, while Bob rubbed against her legs. They were lots of company for her, as they played a game of hide and seek when the grass got up high enough so they could hide in it. One would go and hide, and the other one would find him, then they would race back to her and the other one go. The one left would wait until he thought the other had time to hide, then go and find him. They'd keep this up until they got tired out running.

Most of the claims above us were worked out and the owners gone. Old Michael [M.] Hogan had a claim well up the creek. He could not make wages as he was above where the coarse gold came in, but he hung on. A man name Kate White came in that spring and staked a claim above Hogan's. But I think his idea was to try to find the ledge that the gold came out of, as we could see him often over the mountain roaming around. He had two very large dogs and a good gun.

One day a big silvertip bear came around the mountain on the other side of the creek and he killed it. He brought us down some of the meat and gave the other boys all they wanted of it.

Perkins came up and lived in his tent, and as I remember just the three of us worked that summer, as I knew we could work out the cut by freeze-up time. We did finish it September 23, two days before freeze-up. The boys helped me take the boxes down and pile them up, and then left, as they did not think there would be work the next year. I thought I could make wages for a year or two longer, as the rim on the other side of the creek was left, and had some gold in it. It would be hard to work, so I planned to get Perkins to help me work it out, as two were all that could work on the small strip. We stayed there awhile and shot birds, but walked down before it began to snow. Mrs. Morgan had got to be a good walker climbing around up there shooting birds. As I remember, we put Bob in the packsack and I carried him down to the cabin in Sunrise.

Miner bathing in a length of sluice box, Sixmile drainage, 1898.
PHOTOGRAPH COURTESY OF DONALD CLICKNER, TROY, NEW YORK.

CHAPTER 9

A WINTER HUNTING TRIP WITH CHARLEY YORK

It looked like a long winter ahead but did not turn out that way. Sometime in November, [Charles E.] Charley York asked me if I knew where we could get a moose. York was a small man who had come from Pacific County, Washington, the spring of '98. Since then he had been prospecting around and using up most of his money. I told him that I thought there would be moose over in the Johnson and Lake[1] creeks that emptied into the upper end of Kenai Lake. There had been no gold in these creeks and so no white men in there of late. He said that if he could get part of a moose he could make it through the winter, as he had a good cabin where he stayed during the winters.

He wanted me to go with him and get a moose. I told him it was a long way over there and it would be more work to get the meat out if we got one than it was worth. Besides, it would be a hard, cold trip then. But he kept after me, saying we would not be doing anything all winter, and a trip over there would not hurt us, whereas it might mean his life if we could get a moose. I finally agreed to go with him, and I borrowed a good rifle from old Fred Smith. It was a 30-40 Winchester and boy, that gun could shoot. I had never seen a gun coated with nickel before. Maybe he had it made to order.

I don't know yet how I happened to be foolish enough to go on a trip of that kind that time of year in a country like that. But I did, and we went up to my cabin at the mine, as we had plenty of grub and blankets there to keep us warm. The day we got up there it started snowing, light, flaky snow that would settle down in time, but was not good to be out in. We waited a few days until it quit, and packed up enough grub we thought to last us a week. We rolled the blankets up in a canvas I had and struck out. We got up the East Fork to the little lake on the divide and camped in that bunch of timber there. It was cold nights, so I let Mage sleep under

---

1   Lake Creek is now known as Trail Creek.

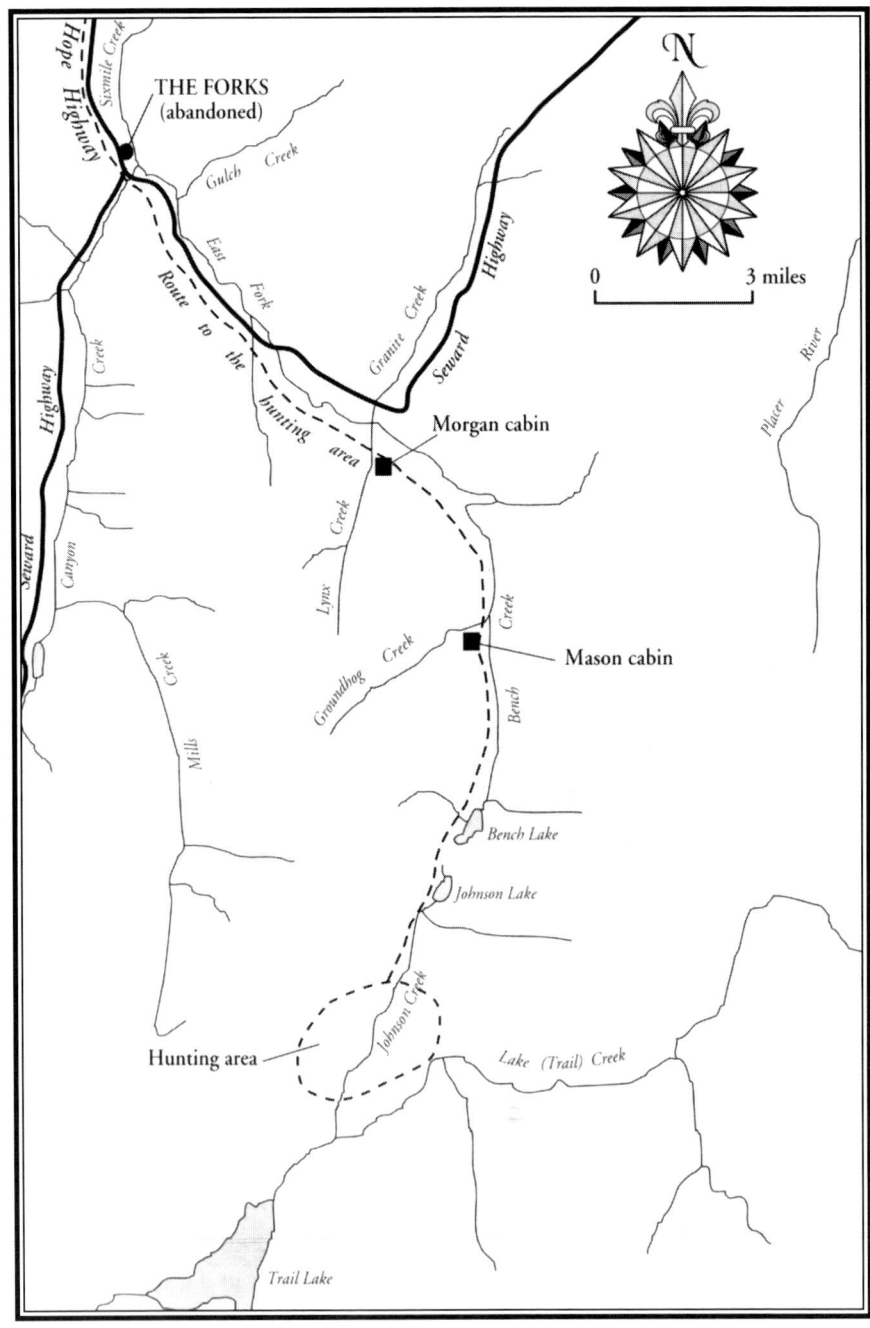

Map of Jack Morgan's winter hunting trip, late 1900, showing the location of present-day Seward and Hope highways.

the blankets beside me as he had short hair, but we all slept cold before morning. We went on by the lake and down Johnson Creek quite a way.

Finally, we saw tracks of a moose cow and calf and followed them, as they went through a very low divide between Johnson and Lake creeks. In the saddle we could see it was only a short distance to Lake Creek. The spruce timber was thick, about piling size, and lots of the smaller trees were dead and would make good wood for us to camp by. I told York we would cut our wood about six feet long, build our fire where our bed would be, get our meal and cut sticks, then move the fire across the foot of the bed. We cut down a green spruce to get boughs to put over the coals when we moved the fire, then spread the canvas over the boughs, and put our blankets over the canvas. The heat came up so that we slept good and warm all night. I had never heard of this before, but have read an article in a magazine since, that a hundred years ago the French Canadians did this to sleep warm when they were out winters. Anyway, we slept good and warm from then on. I cut some logs off the green spruce and put them on the fire so they would burn slowly all day and we would have no trouble starting a fire if we came in late.

We followed the moose tracks on down to a little beaver dam that was frozen over with ice at least a couple of inches thick. The moose had walked over it and we followed them out to the creek. They crossed it and walked into a spruce and willow flat where it was so thick that we could not see very far. The willows had been eaten down by the moose each year so they would sprout up and get about two or three feet high. The spruce had got set in so they made a regular roof over the willows. It was a regular moose heaven. The cow and calf had bedded down several times. Their tracks were fresh and we followed them. But they had spotted us and went around and around.

I was ahead and finally, when I did not hear York, I looked around and he was not near me. I whistled, and he did not answer. Finally I hollered and he did not answer me. He had brought my shotgun loaded with cartridges with buckshot in them. I thought he might take me for a moose in that dark place so I went as straight as I could out to the place where we came into the thicket. There was a mile or more along the river that was open. I looked across the open flat and saw the cow and calf just going into the timber on the other side. I yelled again for York but got no response, so I went after the cow and calf. They went up through the timber and into another willow pasture on a big flat. I followed them around a little while, but knew it was no use, as it was getting late then, and I was worried about York.

Finally I went on back to where we had crossed the creek on a drift, but Charley had not come back that way. So I yelled several times and still got no answer. I thought he might have got across the creek below there and gone on up to the camp, so I started back. It had not got any warmer, but I suppose the moose and our weight must have bent the ice down so it touched the water and softened it. As I started back across the little lake the ice broke and let me down in the water. I could break the ice down with my left elbow and held the gun up in my right hand and kept breaking it down until I felt bottom with my feet. Mage was behind me and did not go in when the ice broke. But he saw I was in trouble and jumped in and swam up beside me and tried to put his head under my right arm to hold me up. I finally broke the ice to where it was shallow, crawled out and pulled Mage out.

We hurried up to the camp, found the fire still burning and piled on a lot of dry wood and soon had a roaring fire. I pulled my clothes off and wrung them out the best I could and put them back on as I had no change. Then I looked into the gun and saw I had not got any water or mud in it, so shot a couple of times in the air, but got no answer. I was worried about York then, but I had to stay right by the fire and keep turning around and around to keep warm and dry my clothes.

Soon York came walking in on the trail we went out on. He asked me what I was shooting at. I told him I was shooting so he could hear me as I thought he was lost. I asked him if he heard me whistling and yelling for him, and he said he had heard me but was so near the moose that he did not want to make any noise. He said he followed them all day but did not get in sight of them. I asked him if he came over the little lake and he said he came to it, saw the ice all broken in and went around it. He got supper while I was keeping warm and drying out.

We got an early start next morning and went around the edge of the flat to where a big spring came out of the mountain and ran almost straight to the river. It was ten feet across and six inches deep. The water was so warm that no ice had frozen in it or on it. A big mallard duck and a drake rose up out of the spring, flew down a way and lit in the stream. I told York to take the buckshot out of the gun and put in fine shot cartridges. He did, and handed the gun to me saying he could not hit them flying. I took the gun and replied that we needed them so bad that they were not going to get to fly! I slipped down along the stream and when they got together I got both of them with the one shot. We hung them up in a bush and went on to the willow thicket.

I told York that one of us should hide there near where the moose went in while the other followed them around until they came out, since they would no doubt come out near where they went in. But he said he knew he could not kill them with the shotgun and besides, he wasn't going to get out of sight of me as he was afraid he would get lost again. I knew then he had been lost in the other thicket. But I had to admire his complacency in being so cool and calm when he got to the camp.

We followed the moose around quite awhile, and finally tracked them to where they came out in the exact spot where they and we had gone in. They had gone back in our tracks within ten feet of our fire on their way back to Johnson Creek.

It started snowing again and kept it up, but we had the ducks for supper. We had to boil them, but they were big and fat and I don't believe I ever tasted anything as good as those stewed ducks. The snow was still coming down so thick next morning that we could not see far. So I told York that he should stay in camp and cut all the dry wood we would need for the night while I followed the moose over to Johnson Creek and tried to locate them.

Their tracks had been snowed over, but I knew they would keep in the old moose trail that they and we had come over. So I went on over to the creek. It was wide there on a riffle so that I could wade it without getting water over the top of my boots. I went on out into timber and soon came to a willow pasture where the cow had got into a big band of moose. Their tracks were fresh and I could see they were headed up the creek. I followed along, until I finally came up to them and heard them snort and run, but the snow was coming down so thick that I could not see them. There was no use following them any further, so I went back to camp.

The snow was getting so deep that I was getting worried as we had eaten more than we figured we would. The bacon was gone, our flour was about gone, and we could not see to shoot the grouse. We had a little rice left, some sugar, and plenty of salt. We used all the flour making hot cakes for breakfast. The snow had piled up nearly to our forks. But it was fine and soft, that is, dry and what you might call powdery, so one could press through it. However, it would tire us in time. I told York that we would start home as it was beginning to look desperate. He said he hated to go back without a moose, and I said I did too, but it was better to go without a moose than not to go at all. I rolled up the blankets and carried them and he carried the cooking outfit and the little grub we had left. I took the lead and broke trail and kept in the timber as the snow did not seem to be so deep there.

It was slow going. But we worried along until I think about one o'clock when it quit snowing and got lighter, like it was going to clear up. We were on a high point and I went out to the edge of it where it looked to be nearly a hundred feet down to the creek. It was light enough so we could see across the flat on the other side, and there was a band of at least a dozen moose on the far side of the flat feeding in a willow pasture along the foot of the hill.

Wild Alaska moose.
JOHN BROOKS COLLECTION, UNIVERSITY OF ALASKA/FAIRBANKS.

I took my pack off and loaded the rifle and asked York how far he thought they were away. He said too far to shoot. I said I thought it was about three hundred yards, and set the sights for that distance. The snow was so deep in the willows that it seemed to come up about halfway on the animals. I picked out the one that looked like he had the biggest horns, and pulled down on him. I could not see that he fell, and York said he did not. So I pulled down on the one with the biggest horns again, and we could not see that he fell either. They scattered in every direction then, and I saw a small bull start up the creek, but he turned and came down.

I said: "That's the one I want."

He came within a hundred yards of us. I pulled down on him and he fell, but tried to get up and started to try to crawl away. I saw that I had only broken his back, and thought then of having the sights raised. I lowered the sights and shot him in the neck and finished him. York was wild with delight.

We had to go up the creek about a half mile to get by the bluff. When we got down to the creek, we found a drift we could cross on. When we got down to the moose, York was so happy he was almost drunk with good cheer. I told him to go and make camp in the edge of the timber and cut a lot of wood, as it was getting colder. I took the entrails out of the moose, as I knew if they were left in the animals overnight the meat would be ruined no matter how cold it was. When I got him cleaned out and got the liver and a lot of tallow to fry the liver in, I went up to where York was making camp and told him I was going up to where I first shot at them, as I might have hit them. He laughed and said the bullet did not go halfway to them.

I went anyway, and found two big bulls lying there shot through right where I aimed at them. I took their entrails out, then reported to York that we were in for it, as we would have to skin them out in the morning and build a cache for the meat. We could come back after the creeks froze over in January and sled the meat out, as it would be a crime to let it waste there.

York went to cutting down a bunch of young cottonwoods. He cut the lengths about ten feet and the cross ends about six feet long. I skinned the moose out good, and was surprised that they were still warm in the morning. I then cut them up, and dragged the quarters down to where we were going to build the cache. The next morning we put the poles in shape to make a floor for the cache and then built up the sides. We put the quarters in as we built up the sides. When we got it high enough to hold all of the meat we covered it over, put the hides over the cache, then put brush on top of the skins. Of course, we kept some of the choicest meat to eat and some to take with us. We had a bucket big enough to cook a tongue in, and had a tongue cooking each night. We cut out a big ten-derloin and fried it in hot moose fat. Even Mage ate tenderloin steaks. He lived high while we were there.

It was lucky that we had lots of salt, as our rice was gone and we had straight meat the last day and night. We started back to Lynx Creek the morning after we got the meat cached. The snow had settled down some after it quit snowing, and was not so deep but a little hard to pull through. We worried along and got over to Groundhog Creek in the late afternoon. I told York that we would go up to [Charley] Mason's cabin as he had told me that if I was ever up there to make myself at home. He had a good stove in the cabin, lots of dry wood in the wood-shed and blankets in a box where the mice and wood rats could not get at them. He had gone to Nome with Waskey the year before.

York said: "Oh, heck, let's go on to your cabin."

He thought we could find the way if it did get dark, but I told him my legs were about played out as it was hard work breaking trail. He said he would break trail the rest of the way, as he felt fresh enough to go clear on to Sunrise that night. He got ahead and started breaking trail. I was not paying any attention to him, and he got off the trail and wound up in the brush. I took the lead and got us back onto the trail, but he said that it was too hard breaking trail and he could not do it any longer. He thought he could follow me if I could make it. I had got rested up a little, so I went ahead. Just as it was getting dark he said he'd have to stop, as he was getting sick. He suggested leaving the meat and gun there and coming back for them in the morning. I told him that maybe we had better build a fire and stay there as it was still light enough to see to cut wood. But he said he could make it without the pack, and did not think it was much farther. However, it was farther than he thought, and when we got down to the big open flat above Lynx Creek he said he could not go any farther.

I put the blankets down and told him to sit on them while I cut down a little dead spruce. Again he suggested that if I could find my way from there to the cabin he was sure he could make it on in, so we started again. I had the ax in one hand, the rifle in the other, all the blankets on my back, and was towing York by the pack rope. It was light enough then so I could see the green timber at Lynx Creek, and I went slow.

I knew there was a hole about eight feet deep on that side of the creek where someone had sunk it to prospect the gravel. I knew where it was, and that the trail went around just below it. But when we got in the green timber it was so dark I could not see much. I missed my bearings and walked right into the hole. York came in on top of me. I let go of the gun and ax to try to keep from landing on my head. Neither one of us was hurt, as there was enough soft snow in the hole to break the fall.

We shook ourselves off and I shoved him up to where he could crawl on out. Then I found the gun and ax and handed them to him and got the end of the rope loose that the blankets were tied with. I climbed onto the end of the blankets with the end of the rope and got up far enough so I could climb out. Then pulled the blankets out after me. We straightened things out and started again. When we got across the creek we found that someone had gone up the creek after it had quit snowing and had made a fairly good trail from there on.

York had been complaining of being thirsty, and when we came to a little open place in the creek he said he had to get a drink. He lay down and started drinking and just kept on drinking. I told him to stop, and when he did not I got him by the collar and dragged him away from the water. He soon began to vomit and was awfully sick. I knew I could carry him from there on as it was less than a half mile, but he said just to let him rest a little while and he could make it. He did, but he was crying and fell over on the bed when we got in the cabin. I built a good fire in the stove and soon had some water boiling. I dug the whiskey bottle out of the cellar and made a hot toddy for each of us. When I took his to him he raised up and told me he never had taken a drink of whiskey.

He tasted it, then drank it all, looked at the cup and said: "God bless you, I feel lots better already, and my stomach does not feel sick now."

Next morning, he seemed about normal and after a good breakfast he said he was going back to get the meat and things and the gun where we left them. I told him I would go and get them, but he said it was his job as he felt as well as he ever had. Away he went and was back with them by noon. The next day we went on to Sunrise, and told them of the hard job we had made for ourselves.

We took in the Christmas fun and when the creeks froze over in January, 1901, sledded the meat in. It's not a very hard job for two fellows to make a sled trail after the snow gets about two feet deep. York went ahead with the snowshoes. The two sleds were tied together and Mage and I pulled them right along behind him. Over low places crossing some of the little creeks we would throw some brush and shovel snow on it to make a fairly decent trail. When we got up to the little bunch of timber by the lake, we shoveled the snow away under the trees, set up the tent, and cut down some trees for wood. We trimmed the boughs and covered the ground in the tent, then cut enough wood to keep a fire going all night in the little stove.

Next morning, when we got down to our meat cache we found that we need not have built a cache at all, as the wolves had tramped down the snow all around the cache and had gone within about thirty feet of it, but no further. Some of them had been trapped, we supposed, and were afraid there were traps around the cache. It took us several days to sled the meat about halfway to the Lynx Creek cabin. Then we went down to the cabin and brought it on down to Lynx Creek. From Lynx Creek we sledded it to Sunrise.

While camped in the tent, we knew it got awfully cold. Mage would cramp and fall over in his harness. I would rub him until he would get over it and jump in and go again. We let him sleep between us at night, and when the fire would burn low in the stove, one of us would get up and fill the stove with wood again. When we left there, it had turned warm enough so we could take our gloves off to tie a rope to hold the load on the sleds. Before that we had to keep our fur gloves on to keep our hands from freezing.

The morning after we got to the Lynx Creek cabin, a couple of the boys from up the creek came up from The Forks and asked us how cold it got up there. We told them we did not know how cold it was where we were camped as we had no thermometer with us, but that it was only twenty-four degrees below when we got to the cabin the night before. They said it was lucky that we did not have a thermometer, as we might have frozen to death if we had known how cold it was.

It was fifty-three degrees below down at The Forks, and no doubt several degrees lower up on the summit where we were camped.

York took about a third of the meat, which gave him plenty to use and some to sell. I gave Fred Smith a quarter, as I appreciated the loan of his hard shooting gun. We gave some to the neighbors and sold some. To our surprise, the meat was all good and tender. An old hunter told me that he thought it was because we had left the skins on the moose overnight and let it cool off slowly. He said that practically all who killed moose would skin and dress them as soon as they killed them, and he thought cooling off so fast made the meat tough. Ours was the only meat we got up there that was not tough.

CHAPTER 10

THE LAST SEASON ON TURNAGAIN ARM

Our good neighbors, Jack and Nellie Frost had a fine baby boy come to them that winter. Mrs. Morgan helped take care of it and felt like she had an interest in it. Of course, everyone loves a baby, and they were so rare up there that I think nearly everyone felt that they had an interest in the two that were born there. We stayed there until along in March and the weather was nice then. We decided to go up to the mine as we had that quarter of moose meat up there, and the ptarmigan hunting would be good. It was nice to have ptarmigan for a change occasionally.

One morning some of the boys going by brought a note from the Frosts stating that their baby was very sick. They wanted us to come down so Mrs. Morgan could help with it. The trail was fine then, and we hooked Mage to the sled and fixed a seat for Mrs. Morgan to sit on. Mage and I went down in a long trot, and we were in Sunrise in a few hours. The dear little boy got worse and passed away in a few days.

View of Sunrise from the east side of Sixmile Creek, late 1890s.
PHOTOGRAPH COURTESY OF THE HOPE AND SUNRISE HISTORICAL SOCIETY.

I helped to dig his little grave down on Point Comfort, where a few others had been buried. It was a beautiful spot, as you could look out over the Arm from there and also up the other way and see all over the little town. The point was covered with white snow during winters and with lovely wild flowers during the spring and summer. If I had to be buried I think it is there where I would want it to be. I believe everyone in town came down when we buried the little fellow. I don't remember who read the burial service, but I remember that we sang "God be with you till we meet again" as the grave was filled and I don't believe there was a dry eye in the whole crowd.

We decided to stay down a few days to do what we could to console the parents of the little boy. A few days later someone came from up the creek and said that five men had been killed in a snow slide up on Lynx Creek. And they were bringing them down for burial on Point Comfort. I helped dig a big grave for them near where the baby was resting. It was quite a job to dig a grave there during the winter as the ground was frozen five or six feet deep then. Of course, everyone knew everyone else in the small town, and this cast a gloom over the town that was hard to forget.

The names of those killed were Dick Lane, Ulysses Graham, [Harry] Hank Willoughby, Michael Hogan, and Fred Shackleford. They were all fine men. They had taken up a load of supplies to that place where Clark worked the Smith ground, and the tents were all still there. They had leased the ground from Smith. The snow was much deeper that year than it had been any year before while we were there. It turned warm the afternoon they got there, and the snow starting melting.

About ten o'clock a slide came down off the mountain on the other side of the creek from our place, poured over the bluff and covered the tents. Frank Flaherty and Gill Devoe were there too. Frank was in the tent with Lane and Graham. He was small and did not get hurt. He said that Lane told him to try to dig his way out and go for help, as he could not move and his back was broken. Graham never spoke. Frank finally got out and found his way down to the Silvertip [Creek] cabin where some men were staying. Some of them went to The Forks for help, and there was a big crowd there by morning. The slide was on the claim adjoining ours and was in sight of our cabin. The men went up to our cabin and cooked and ate there, as we had plenty of everything including what was left of the quarter of moose meat. We were glad that they could get food while digging the boys out.

Gill Devoe was in the tent with the old man Hogan. The walls of the tent were built up with logs a few feet. Gill said the old man was sitting on the bed facing the slide, which shoved him over backwards but did not kill him instantly. Gill could hear him praying for quite awhile. Gill fell where there was considerable space open and someway there was enough air in there to keep him alive until they dug him out.

We had left Bob there and left food for him, and he could get to the moose meat, too, if he needed it. We were shocked over the catastrophe, and did not go back to the claim for quite awhile. When we got there Bob was not there. We imagined that their dogs ran him away, and they no doubt finished up the moose meat as it was all gone when we got back.

Grave markers at the Point Comfort cemetery of the five
victims of the 1901 snow slide on Lynx Creek.
ALASKA HISTORICAL COLLECTIONS, ALASKA STATE LIBRARY, JUNEAU.

Mrs. Morgan was nervous, as we could look right down to where the slide hit the boys, and she did not want to stay there any longer. [J. G.] Tom Fields and [John H.] Bosen Brown offered me a few hundred [250] dollars for my interest in the claim, and [on June 14th] we let them have it with everything including the groceries we had there. We did not get away for a few days, and Mr. Wible rode up one morning on one of his mules to ask me if I would go and work for him on his Canyon Creek mine. He said he had always heard that I could get more work out of men than anyone in the country, and that he would give me the going wages and board Mrs. Morgan, too, if we would go. He had a big cook tent and a cook.

We had the pack train take our tent down to his camp, and we moved down later. We had dug a cellar under the floor of the cabin the fall of '98, and had a hole in the bottom of it to hold a little bucket to put our sacks of gold in. We kept it covered over so we were sure no one would find it while we were away. We kept our canned goods in the cellar so they would not freeze in the winter. We got our gold out of the cellar and put it in the safe at the U. S. Mercantile store in Sunrise, then went up to Canyon Creek where I went to work for Mr. Wible.

Simon Wible's hydraulic operation on the bench, upper right, on the east side of lower Canyon Creek.

F. H. MOFFIT #110, U. S. GEOLOGICAL SURVEY, DENVER, COLORADO.

I think Wible came to Sunrise in '98 in the big rush. He lived in California and had mined in the gold camps there. He was a civil engineer and had located [on] some of the flat below the mouth of Gulch Creek. He ran a ditch from Gulch Creek around the mountain so as to get more water pressure on his ground. He sank a pit and put pipes in so the water would shove the gravel up to his boxes. It worked all right, but there was not enough gold in the gravel to make it pay. The main trouble was there were too many boulders on all the wash in that country. Even up on the high mountains there were big washed boulders.

Wible bought a few of the worked out claims on Canyon Creek and located the flat [bench] above the creek. The flat was around a hundred feet above the creek bed and he could roll his boulders over the bluff. He brought a ditch around from a little creek and had two foot pipe to bring the water to the giants where we could pipe it into the gravel, and, boy, that pressure made the boulders roll over the bank. I worked there until late in September when we went back to Sunrise and got ready to go out on the September boat. Wible was a fine old man. He was 72 then, and got around about as good as any of us. He would go home when it froze up in the fall and come back in the spring.

Jerry O'Dale worked for him and took care of things during the winters. Jerry was a wonderful worker and as fine a man as ever lived. He told me that he went into the Inlet the spring of '95. A man named [Frank] Dusy organized a bunch of men at Fresno, California, and they chartered a sailing schooner and loaded down with the supplies they would need. They each put in what money they could, bought as much stuff as they could pay for, and took it on the boat. When they got there each got his own stuff, and each paid his share toward chartering the schooner.

Jerry told me also that a little sailing boat sailed from Juneau with about a dozen miners and prospectors. Among them was Sam Mills, who had been in the Yukon country and came out over the White Pass, [Benedict C.] Ben Pilcher, Mr. [William E.] Hunt, the Beady brothers [William F., George R. and Alonzo "Lon" Beady], and many others. Jerry said they saw this little schooner coming out of the Arm while their boat was anchored at Fire Island. They all landed at Hope first, but finding everything staked on Bear Creek and Resurrection Creek, they went on up to Sixmile River.

For the early staking of claims in the Hope and Sunrise districts, I rely on Jerry O'Dale's memory, as he was in the area about three years earlier than I was. Jerry said that George Donaldson went across the mountain from Resurrection Creek and down onto Canyon Creek and located the best claim on Canyon Creek. Sam Mills had evidently taken the lead and gone up Canyon Creek to Mills Creek, which was named for him. He saw and prospected the ground that the Polly Mining Company took and told the men that took it how to get up there and find it.

Nearly everyone who was in there then staked claims on Canyon and Mills creeks that fall. Donaldson gave his three partners an interest in his claim. They put in a wing dam, sawed out timber for boxes, sluiced three or four weeks before the freeze-up, and found good pay. Jerry staked a claim above them, but he could not do much alone, and he packed for them and others. They built cabins at Sunrise and sledded up supplies for the next year. He said there were only twenty-eight of them wintered in Sunrise in 1895-96. Sam Mills had a cabin on his claim at The Forks, and Mike [Mekkel] Gladhaugh built a good, warm cabin at Mills Creek. He and old man [Frank] LaMoure had claims on Mills Creek about six miles above the Polly Mine.

The river was slow freezing up that year, so they ran low on food, and LaMoure got a bad case of scurvy. Gladhaugh got scared and went to Sunrise for help. The snow was deep and loose, and he had to break trail all the way on his snow shoes, and had to rest a day before starting back. He told them that he felt sure that LaMoure would be dead by the time they could get back, and if a couple of them would go up and help bury him they could have his claim. Jerry O'Dale and Donaldson went with Mike, taking only small packs of such groceries as they thought LaMoure would need.

It took them two hard days to reach the cabin, and when they got there they found LaMoure about well. He remembered reading that tea from cottonwood bark would cure the scurvy, so he went out in the yard and peeled a lot of the inside bark from a cottonwood tree, boiled it down and drank it every hour all day, and it cured him. They were glad that they did not have to bury LaMoure, if for no other reason than it was a hard job to dig a grave in that frozen ground. Mike insisted on showing them his and the old man's claims, located up in that big flat where the old Major and I prospected in '97.

Someone told LaMoure later that O'Dale and Donaldson had gone up with Mike to help bury him, and were to get his claim in payment. The old man was fighting mad, and he asked Donaldson if that was true.

Donaldson, who liked a joke, said: "Yes, but when we saw your claim we knew it was no good, so we would not go through with the job."

O'Dale told me that he and Donaldson's bunch sledded up supplies for the summer and sawed out lumber. Then he and Donaldson went on hunting trips and looked over the country to see if there were any places they might want to prospect later on. He worked just enough on his claim to do the assessment work each spring, and worked for Donaldson and his partners that summer. I think that Jerry built a cabin in Sunrise that winter, as cabins would sell then. Jerry could do almost anything, and was a kind, pleasant fellow who could get a job anywhere. I mentioned that he worked for Wible the summer I worked there. When Wible found that Jerry was reliable and dependable, he got him to take care of things that winter and work for him the next summer.

The fall of 1896, Jerry told me, W. [William] G. Jack, [Christopher] Chris Spillum, and Paul Buckley took a year's supplies by boat up the famous Susitna River as far as the Alaska Commercial Company station and camped there until the snow got deep enough to sled it on up the river to where they thought they should begin to prospect. They stayed there until the ice got out of the river so they could begin prospecting. They found little encouragement, as they did not find gold in the river. But they worked on up the river to where little creeks came in. They did find some fine colors in the creek gravel, but not enough to pay to work. I don't know just how far up they got, and I don't believe they knew, for they quit before freezing time and went over to Sunrise. That was the fall of '97, and they were in Sunrise before I left, but I did not meet them.

[Ralph] Oldham, [Dante] Barton, [Charles J.] Brooks, [Thomas] Fritz Fenstermacher, and several others came to Sunrise that fall, but I do not know how late. With Chris Spillum's help they located nine claims on Crow Creek, across the Arm from Sunrise. Brooks was no doubt a good attorney, as he drew up a contract that held the claims together. The outfit was known as the Crow Creek Consolidated Mine. That was the first of January, 1898. The creek went vacant then, and Chris was the only one who could buck the snow and get to the ground to post their notices, as the snow was much deeper on that side of the Arm that year. They sawed out lumber for boxes and worked the ground that year, but there were not many of the nine that could do a good day's work shoveling gravel.

As stated, Brooks was an attorney, and was getting along in years, and Oldham, who had taught school all his life, was in his forties. He was big and fat, so you may know that he could not do much. Barton was also an attorney, but had worked as a reporter on a Kansas City paper and was very frail, anyway. Jack, another one of the partners, had been a salesman in a store in San Francisco, and of course the work was new to him. Fenstermacher was no doubt willing, but they said it kept him busy telling the others what to do. I do not remember the other partners' names, but it seems that Chris and Buckley were the only ones who could do a real day's work. They did not take out much gold, and of course there were disagreements among them. However, some of them did the assessment work the next year to hold it together.

Waiting for the boat at Sunrise was pleasant, as the weather was ideal. Looking through the glasses, I could see sheep feeding on the mountain on the west. Looking east across the creek, I saw a cow moose eating the grass tops along a trail the moose had around the mountain. We all had thought the moose and sheep had been killed off around there, but these had come back.

H. A. Smith, who ran the Alaska Commercial Company store, asked me to go up to Mills Creek and serve some papers on a self-organized company which had got some pipe and lumber up on Mills Creek on the vacant ground that the Major and I prospected, and was going to pipe the gravel into the boxes. Mr. Fenstermacher, a Mr. Code, and John Blaugh were the operators.

The first Crow Creek Mine partners, circa 1898: Left to right, Charles Brooks, Dante Barton, unidentified, Fritz Fenstermacher, and Ralph Oldham.
Photograph courtesy of *Alaska Sportsman.*

Frank Fleeharter was working in the store with Smith, and I asked why he did not send Frank as they were not very busy. He said he wanted service on them, and he was afraid they would talk Frank out of it, but knew I would make them acknowledge service. I went, and sure enough, they started to tell me it was all right as they would fix it up with Smith and everything was coming along good.

I said: "Yes, that's all right, but you must sign this paper acknowledging service, as that is what I came for, and I will not go back without it."

Code was a nice fellow. And since he was head of the company he went down with me to sign the paper, if Smith insisted on it.

The next day Smith wanted me to go over to Bird Creek and tack up some notices on some property there. His company had backed some outfit that worked some of the ground but could not make it pay, so went away and left everything. I think that Brooks, the attorney there, had handled the matter. The company had bid on the property and was giving notice to anyone who might try to take the pipe and stuff away that the company now owned it and would protect it.

"Copper River" was working for Smith then, and he took me over in a good sail boat. We got over into Bird Creek in good time, and he said he wanted to go bear hunting. I told him to be back there by four PM, as the tide would be right for us to go back on. He was there, but the wind had come up and the Arm was getting rough, whitecaps breaking all over it. I told "Copper River" that I thought we had better wait until morning, as the wind would not be blowing then. But he said we would go, as the boat was safe and it would be fun to sail over now.

I did not like it, but I got in the boat and he shoved out into the current and put up the sail. We plowed into the breakers. The spray would fly in his face and he would laugh and yell. It came into the boat so fast that it kept me busy bailing and vomiting, too, as I got awfully seasick. However, we soon got across and he sailed up to the little dock and I got out and hurried home. He tied the boat up and went to the store.

Smith asked him where I was, and "Copper River" said: "He went home. Morgan got Jesus Christ sick."

I remember that Barton went out the fall of '99. I think that some of the partners in the Crow Creek Consolidated Mine sold their interest to others, as the enterprise held together indefinitely. Jack wanted me to buy some of them cheap and take over and run the mine the spring of 1901. But we had already decided to come out that fall, and I did not want to ever cross that Arm again in a small boat. They were all fine fellows in the Crow Creek Consolidated Mine, and did their part in carrying on the entertainments during the winters. Oldham went out the fall of '99.

In a few days the boat was ready to go and we got on it. Mage knew we were going, and thought he was going with us. We knew he belonged to that country. I gave him to H. A. Smith, who was still running the Alaska Commercial

Company store in Sunrise. There were a number going on the boat, and everyone in town came down there to see us off. Smith was sitting down on the wharf, and I told him he would have to hold Mage.

The Bertha *taking on freight.*
AMELIA ELKINTON COLLECTION, UNIVERSITY OF ALASKA FAIRBANKS.

When we got on the boat, Mage pulled loose from him and came to me and reared up on me. I had put a little piece of rope in my pocket to tie him, as I anticipated this. I tied the rope around his neck and gave it to Smith. I stooped over and hugged Mage, and told him to be good, as we had to leave him. I hurried back on the boat as they were taking the ropes off then, and I could not look back at Mage. It was two miles down the river to the Arm proper and there was a long sand spit that ran down between the river and the Arm which the tide had not covered yet.

When we were running into the Arm, someone said: "There comes Mage."

I looked, and there he came running down the spit barking. He went into the water until his head only stuck up, and he was howling with a broken heart. Smith had turned him loose too soon. I choked up and went to the other side of the boat and felt hot tears roll down my face. We were getting almost out of hearing when I looked back and could just see his head above the water. I wished then that he was on the boat, but it was too late.

"Colonel" Revelle rode on the boat we came out on as far as Seward. When we got on the boat at Tyonek, he came up to our room and said he had the room under ours on the lower deck, and his room was full of watermelons. He wanted to know if I had a small rope, and I did have one. He said to let it down and he would tie the biggest melon to it. When he gave the rope three jerks, I was to pull up the melon and we would all get together in our room and eat it. That is, of course, if we could get it up before the steward came to move the melons. It worked all right, and did that melon taste good—the first in five years.

When Mrs. [Nellie] Frost came into the room, she said: "Where did you get that fine melon?"

The Colonel said: "The steward gave it to us."

And she said: "Well, wasn't that nice of him."

And the Colonel said: "Yes, it was, but don't thank him for it, as he doesn't know it yet."

Colonel Revelle stayed there at Seward and married one of the Lowell girls [Eva] and raised a big family. He passed away there many years later.

Mrs. Frost came out with us as far as Seattle. Mr. and Mrs. [Charles E. "Clint"] Pierce were on the boat, and C. F. Yeaton, who was relieved of his job in the U. S. Mercantile Company store, also came on the trip. This boat anchored at Tyonek, where we had to wait a few days, as the *Bertha* was late.

We finally got to Seattle where we sold our gold. The government had an assay office there by this time to weigh and buy the gold from the Alaska miners. We got only sixteen dollars an ounce for it then. It developed that the man who was running the assay office was taking a little out of each one's gold and had over a hundred thousand dollars in the bank there.

He dipped a little too deep in one man's sack soon after this and was reported to the government. They put a detective in with him as helper. He did not suspect it, and the detective arrested him. He was sent to the pen for several years.

Mrs. Morgan thought we should buy a farm with part of our money, as money had a habit of getting away from people who never had much before. So we bought a farm down on the Yaquina River in Lincoln County, Oregon, and lived there one year. However, it seemed so slow we rented the farm and went back to Willapa and went to logging again.

I wrote to H. A. Smith as soon as we got settled on the farm and asked him about Mage. He wrote me that Mage went back to them, but would go over to our cabin every evening and sit and howl for awhile for about two weeks. All the neighbors would try to comfort him, and he finally seemed satisfied to be in the store.

Jerry O'Dale came out the fall of 1902 and visited all of his folks back in Chicago, where he met the girl he married three years later. If I thought Jerry would read this, I would not write all of it, as he might blush. But he was a friend to everyone he knew, and everyone he knew was his friend. A finer man than Jerry never lived.

CHAPTER 11

WHERE HAVE ALL THE "OLD-TIMERS" GONE?

O n our moose hunt the last winter I was in Sunrise, when York and I were taking care of the moose where we cached the meat, I thought the heads were so nice that I saved the capes[1] and skinned them out nights by the fire. I cleaned the heads and folded the capes up so they proved good, and when we sledded them over to the cabin I salted them so good that they kept. I took them to Seattle on the boat, as I thought they should be saved. A taxidermist named [Christ C.] Berge there in Seattle said he had an order for two good heads. He took the two big ones and the capes. I asked him what he would charge to mount the small head, as I wanted to give one to my old friend John Myers, the druggist at South Bend, Washington. He said he would mount the head, take the other two and give me a hundred dollars, so we settled the deal. I gave him Myers' address and told him to ship the small head to him when he got it done.

About six months later I got a letter from Myers saying the head had arrived, and it was a magnificent thing. He had pictures taken of it and sent one to me. That is the only thing I have left now of that moose hunt, but through all the years I have kept track of many of the "old timers."

Fred Smith took a couple of the boys that worked for him and went over into the Copper River country prospecting the spring of 1901, the year we came out. I heard afterward that during the fall of that year Fred got tired, sat down, leaned back against a tree, went to sleep and froze to death. He was getting well along in years then, and I imagine that was the way he wanted to go. I understood that his widow, the former Mrs. White, stayed there in Sunrise and kept boarders for for awhile. She went to Anchorage when the railroad was built in there, put up a lodging house, and ran it until she passed away several years later.

---

1 The pelts from the animals' head, neck, and forepart of the shoulders, used for mounting as a trophy.

Oldham went out the fall of '99, but went back later to the Crow Creek Mine and helped carry on until they sold the ground for a good price. He stayed at Anchorage until he died there several years later. Brooks went down to a little town on the north side of the Inlet, where I think he got some kind of government job. He stayed there until he passed away.

When H. A. Smith decided to quit the store in Sunrise, he wrote me that he gave Mage to John Brownlow, who was very fond of him.

Brownlow had located a placer claim on a little stream that ran into Kenai Lake. He worked on it summers and came to Sunrise to winter, as there were no stores over there then. Just one family lived on the Sound where Seward is now.

Smith came to Seattle to find work. His wife [Mary R. Smith] and daughter were to stay at Sunrise until he got settled. But he died very suddenly in a park at Seattle a few days after he got there. John Blaugh married the daughter and took her and Mrs. Smith back to his home in Minneapolis. I never heard anything more from them.

Tramway from Sunrise to the dock near the mouth of Sixmile Creek.
JOHN BROOKS COLLECTION, UNIVERSITY OF ALASKA FAIRBANKS.

The man who relieved Yeaton at the U. S. Mercantile Store in Sunrise sold off what goods were left, locked the store, and came back to Seattle. Mr. Yeaton bought the building very cheap and took up a stock of goods, as he had learned that the Alaska Commercial Company was also going to close their store. Wheeler never came back. Wallace closed his stock out and went to Nome.

Waskey had located a claim on that rich Anvil Creek at Nome and took out several hundred thousand dollars the first year, or so the story ran. Wallace went up to get his half of it and went back to Minneapolis too, but Waskey stayed on up there and worked some more ground. He became very popular up there, as he was full of energy and aggressive and made friends wherever he was. He was chosen for Alaska's first delegate to Congress, and put in two years [1906-1907] in Washington, D. C. However, he was homesick for Alaska and went back to Nome, located a claim on another creek and spent considerable money operating it. They said it did not turn out good. But he kept busy up there and married a school teacher, I believe. They ran a store in one of the towns on Bristol Bay for awhile, and live in Fairbanks now.

Jerry O'Dale made a trip up there a few years ago and he went all over the country. He flew up to Barrow and stopped at Nome and Fairbanks. But did he not get to see Waskey, as he was out on a prospecting trip when Jerry was there. Jerry said he stopped at Anchorage and Seward and saw all his other old friends that were left up there.

I ran into Mr. Yeaton in Seattle after he came back to Sunrise. He told me that he did not know why he went back to a dying town, except that he liked to be there. Several of the old fellows were still there, and they would snipe around up on the creeks summers and pick up enough to live on winters. He had the only store there then and kept it warm during the winters so they would have a place to loaf and tell yarns. He said old Mr. [Ferdinand] Martin[2] was still there and he kind of looked after him. Martin went up to Boston Bar where someone had left some boxes, and made a few dollars a day washing the gravel and cleaned up three hundred dollars. He batched in Windy's cabin while working up there, and had two fine shepherd dogs that stayed with him.

One day one of the dogs came running into the store. The dog took hold of Yeaton's pants leg and pulled and barked and ran out. The dog ran up the road a way, then came back and did it over again. Yeaton ran over and told some other fellows at a cabin nearby what the dog was doing, and that he was sure Martin

2 The postmaster for Sunrise, 1912-1919.

Frank Waskey, Alaska's first Representative to Congress, 1906-1907.
EARLY PRINTS OF ALASKA, ALASKA HISTORICAL COLLECTIONS, ALASKA STATE LIBRARY, JUNEAU.

was in trouble. They hurried up there as fast as they could. The dog would run
ahead of them, and come back in sight of them and bark, then run ahead again.
I think it was at least five miles up there, and when they got there they found that
a bank of gravel had fallen over on Martin in his cut and had buried him so he
was helpless. He had gotten the gravel away from his face so he could breathe.
He was so weak he could hardly move when they got there. They dug him out

and found that he had no bones broken, but one of the men stayed with him a few days until he got back on his feet.

Yeaton had insured his store and goods for ten thousand dollars. A fire started in the lower end of the little town of Sunrise and the wind drove it up to where it got his store, the Alaska Commercial Company's store, and Wheeler's store and both the old saloon buildings. [Michael] Mike Connolly's cabin was away up the river, so the fire did not reach there, and there were several other cabins that it did not get. Mr. Yeaton got his insurance and did not go back again.

I never knew just how long Tom Fields and Bosen Brown worked our old claim, but I think Mr. Yeaton told me that they were still working there and going down to Sunrise winters. It seems that no one tried to work the Smith and Gale ground after the snowslide killed the boys. Jerry O'Dale told me that [Nathan P.] Nate White located these claims when they became vacant, and ran a tunnel through the little ridge that ran along between the creek and the flat on the other side. The creek was fifty feet or more above the flat, and he put in a flume five or six feet wide and four or five feet high with plenty of fall. He planned to run everything through the flume, boulders and all.

He got some pipe and started piping the gravel and boulders into the flume, and had most of the creek running through the flume. It seemed that the flume choked up at the lower end and filled up solid before he could turn the water off, and that ended his effort. He went away disgusted, a sadder but wiser man.

After Fields and Brown quit, a couple of old fellows went in and located the whole creek and the benches. They made a long ditch and got the water high enough to pipe [hydraulic] the benches off. They took out a little money, but lacked funds enough to rig up and work it right. Finally they advertised it for sale, and a man came up from Los Angeles and bought it for twenty-five hundred dollars. I never knew the man's name, but he took plenty of pipe and lumber to work it right, and had a bunch of men laying pipe on the flat where our cabin stood. There was more snow than usual that year, about six feet deep after it settled, and when it turned warm the snow on the whole mountain on the opposite side of the creek slid clear up to the head of the creek. It filled the creek and ran up on the flat about thirty feet deep, they said, and covered these six men. The owner got enough help to dig them out and bury them. This happened in 1933 or 1934.[3] I don't know whether they took them down to Point Comfort or not, but they

3   The snow slide occurred on May 10, 1937. It swept the entire crew off of a bench claim, carrying them and their equipment 250 feet into the canyon below, taking the lives of David Mansfield, John E. Dyste, Ben Crabtree, Wilbert Zetzman, Einar Pederson, and John Mehus.

probably did, as by that time the government had built a good road up the mouth of Lynx Creek and on over to the Kenai country.

Nathan White's hydraulic operation on Lynx Creek.
SYLVIA SEXTON COLLECTION, SEWARD COMMUNITY LIBRARY AND MUSEUM.

This made eleven men that the gold in Lynx Creek had caused to lose their lives. They said the man that bought the creek went away, no doubt a very much sadder man, and never came back. I can visualize it only as it was when we were there, a beautiful mountain on the opposite side of the creek, covered with grass and wild flowers in the summer and snow in winter. It seemed that we got away at the right time.

I would not want to see it now. I can visualize Sunrise as it was when we were there. There was a high mountain on the southeast side with two very sharp peaks that stood away up high. When the sun came up in winter, it was low enough to go behind one peak for awhile and come out for a short while and then go behind the other until it got past it. That made three sunrises, and that was why the town was called Sunrise.

It's not even a ghost town now, as another fire burned most of the cabins. Mike Connolly wrote me that he burned the rest of them for firewood. He still worked his ground there at the mouth of the canyon and took out enough gold to buy his groceries. Connolly said he trapped some every winter, and that the game also came back. The moose came down in his garden and he had to keep a dog to chase them out nights. As long as he lived, Connolly kept thinking some corporation would come in and buy his ground. He got a lot of nuggets there. A fellow who stayed with Mike awhile one summer told him that another man came in there and told him he knew where he could sell his ground for a good price. The fellow suggested that if he took Mike's nuggets out to show the other man that would cinch the deal. Mike let him take them, about seven hundred dollars worth, and never heard from the fellow again.

I don't remember what year it was that a man here in Portland came into my office one day and said his wife had just returned from Hope. Her brother had a store there, and they had gotten acquainted with Mike. The stage on its way to Hope always stopped at Mike's place at Sunrise to give him his paper and mail. As she was leaving, she stopped to tell Mike goodbye. He gave her my address and told her to be sure to go in and see me and tell me he was still going strong and had a good man helping him to get ready to work his mine that summer.

A few days later the same man came in to my office and said they just got a letter from his brother-in-law at Hope. It said that Mike and his man were trying to stretch an old cable across the river and the boat upset in the current. Mike got tangled in the cable and was drowned before the other fellow got out and got hold of the cable and pulled him out. Mike had written me before that he had passed his 77th milepost and was feeling fine.

My old friend Charley Lockhart had gone north and finally settled in Fairbanks. He located a lot of that deep ground that they worked out with a dredge later. He wrote me from where he was working his assessment on one of his claims that he had just had his 77th birthday. He was feeling as young as ever, and was going to move to another claim soon to do the assessment on it. Sometime later [in 1939] I saw in an Alaskan paper that Charley's partner found him sitting against a rock dead, apparently from heart failure. When I got to my 77th year, I watched my step until my next birthday. But now I have safely passed my 92nd birthday.

Jerry O'Dale told me that when he was on his last trip up to Sunrise, he stopped at Mike's cabin and went down to where the stores and saloon had been. There were cottonwood trees more than a foot thick growing where the street and stores had been, and the brush was so thick he could not get down to old Point Comfort. Mike had written often and urged me to go back and visit him and put in a summer up there. But I had no desire to go back as it was a lovely place when I left. I wanted to remember it that way with the many good, kind-hearted people I knew there. It will remain in my memory as it was then as long as I live.

Sunrise City (date unknown).
SYLVIA SEXTON COLLECTION, SEWARD COMMUNITY LIBRARY AND MUSEUM.

Jerry O'Dale worked in the Girdwood mine on Crow Creek most of the summer of 1903 and 1904. A corporation known as the Alaska Central Railroad moved into Seward about that time and started surveying a line from Seward to Fairbanks. The man in charge was lucky enough to hire Jerry at a good salary as a general handyman. They had three crews on the job, and Jerry said all he had to do was to keep them in touch with each other and with the main office at Seward, and blaze trail for their pack horses. They got the line located the summer of 1905, and the following winter to the Tanana Valley, and a preliminary survey on to Fairbanks.

It was getting along toward September, 1906, when the survey was finished. They kept Jerry on the job gathering up and storing tools and equipment. They gave him a month off to go to Seattle and get married, but told him to hurry back and take care of things, as they had only a few men working along the Arm then. Jerry and his wife were caretakers during the next three years. Then a new company bought the railroad.

Jerry and his wife left Alaska the fall of 1909 and bought a farm near Drain, Oregon. He was just as efficient on the farm as he was in Alaska, and made it pay by raising cattle and goats, while Grace, his wife, raised turkeys and chickens. He bought adjoining land that did not look like it was worth much, but he got it at a low price. He let the young timber grow on it. Grace died many years later, and Jerry sold farm and timber for more than any of the mines in the Turnagain Arm country brought.

He had an urge to see the world then, and went around the world on an English freighter. He would get off and see the country when the boat would stop to unload and load, and had a good time all the way around. Then he bought a home at Sooke, British Columbia, and lived there part of the time. But he put in most of two years flying over northern Canada, where he saw all the gold mines and the oil fields that were worth seeing. Then he flew down to the Hawaiian Islands and finally found a place on one of the islands that he thought had ideal climate. I have forgotten the name of this Island, but he bought a lot in the town of Wailuku and had a house built to suit him, and still lives there. It seems rather remarkable to me now, how we have kept track of each other after we came out from old Sunrise.

Clint and Mrs. Pierce built a lodge at Duckabush, Washington for hunters and fishermen, and maintained it as long as they lived. They had a good business, as Mrs. Pierce was a good cook and Clint a good manager.

Jack Frost came out to Seattle late the fall after we came out, and he and Nellie made their home there for many years. Two fine baby girls came to them there, Virginia and Dorothy. We kept in touch with them and visited back and forth. We found them to be fine people and we had been close friends so long that they seemed almost like kinfolk then. They kept track of those who came out and settled in Seattle. They were later transferred to Spokane, where he was a salesman for the Armour Packing Company until he retired. Their girls graduated from Washington State College, and both took up teaching for awhile.

Jack and Nellie passed away several years ago, but we have kept in touch with the girls ever since. Virginia met and married Earl Cox at Hoquiam, Washington, where he had a grocery store. They made a good team. He ran the store and she still carried on teaching, until two fine sons arrived. They are in college now. The older one is named for her little brother, whom she never knew, who is sleeping on Point Comfort up at old Sunrise. Dorothy has a good job in New York, but comes to Hoquiam to spend her vacation every two years. They drive over to visit us when she is there, as we are getting too old to visit them now.

Mr. Yeaton kept us posted about the Seattle bunch after the Frosts left there. He lived to be 97, and always met me at the hotel when I would go to Seattle. He gathered up a bunch of seven of the old friends one day when I was up there and brought them to the hotel where I was staying. We had a chicken dinner together and put in the afternoon reminiscing on the old days at Sunrise. Mike Connelly kept me posted by letter of those left up there. He knew where they all were and what they were doing, and would write me when one of them passed over the river, up to the time he had to go, too.

CHAPTER 12

OLD FRIENDS AND MEMORIES OF YEARS GONE BY

We moved onto a homestead in the Siletz Reservation in Oregon in 1905. After we had been there two years, a man came in and said he wanted to cruise several quarter sections in there. They told him at Toledo, Oregon, that I knew the country, all the corners well, and I might compass for him. When I went to get a bucket of water he said to Mrs. Morgan: "I know your husband now. He and McEllaney went over in the Kenai country prospecting the winter of '99. They did not find any gold, but caught some marten, mink and fox. When they got back to Sunrise in the spring, I bought their fur to ship out with mine, and in that way I got back to Vancouver, Washington."

He was a good timber cruiser, and was kept busy cruising for the mills and loggers in Washington and Oregon. He and I had a good time telling our experiences in Alaska, and after we moved to Portland, he always came into my office for a little visit when he was in town. His name was Billy Price. He, too, is gone now.

As I was coming down our trail the second year I was on our homestead on the Siletz Reservation, a man sitting by the trail said, "Hello, Alaska!"

I said: "Hello." I looked at him and did not know him.

"You don't remember me," he said, "but I knew who you were as you went by here the other day. You are Lynx Creek Morgan."

"Yes, that's right," I said.

"Well," he said, "I'm Bob McKay, and I was up there with old Joe Wilson and stayed with him a couple of years working some ground on Canyon Creek."

I remembered him then. Old Joe Wilson was a hard drinker and made a lot of noise when they used to come to Sunrise. He stayed in the saloon when he was there, and McKay would get him out of there as soon as he could. I think he held the [gold] sack, and Joe had to go back with him or starve. After Bob McKay left him, Joe had a "one season strike." He continued working for a few years after he cleaned up the pay streak the first year, but could not make enough to pay for grub. Finally, they sent the old fellow over to the government [Pioneer's] home at Sitka, where he spent the rest of his days.

Bob Michaelson went there [the Sitka Pioneer Home] after he worked a few years on the Polly Mine after the others left. Chris Spillum also passed his last days there when he got too old to work. They say that it is a good place for the old worn-out boys, as they have good food and good warm quarters. And there is always enough of them there to interest each other in telling their experiences.

Sunrise, May 2nd, 1906.
Charles Bunnell Collection, University of Alaska Fairbanks.

McKay said that he was building himself a cabin on one of the old soldier claims that had been bought on final certificate, but on which the patent had not been issued. I knew the history of all these claims, and I told him that he would be wasting his time. The law was that when a final certificate was issued, if it was not contested within two years a patent had to be issued.

"Well," he said, "it has not been issued yet, and I'm going to take a gamble on it. I've made good money logging since I came back from Alaska, and a year or two resting will be good for me."

When he learned that it was patented, he laughed and said he would go back to logging and make more money, which he did. He brought his wife and baby over to Newport [Oregon] in a few years to spend their summers.

McKay's reference to Joe Wilson brought to mind the rather amusing incident about Wilson and Potlatch Anderson's wife staking the same claim told earlier.

I don't remember what year the [William D. and Ida C.] Van Siclens came to Sunrise, but they were there two winters. I think Van Siclen had an interest in some property, and it took two years for him to find out that it was no good. He was an architect, and returned to Seattle and built some apartment houses. When I went in to see him he jumped up and grabbed my hand and seemed as glad to see me as I was to see him. He said he could hardly understand how glad he was to see any of the people who were at Sunrise, but that it seemed then that we were something like one big family while we were there.

The year that the Yukon Exposition was in Seattle, I wanted to see the Alaska Exhibit the first thing. When I went in I saw a well dressed man in charge. When I looked at him closely I saw that it was Billy Powers, my first partner on Lynx Creek.

I said, "Hello, Billy, I am glad to see you here."

He stuck out his hand and said: "Who are you?"

And I said: "Your last partner on Lynx Creek, Morgan."

He grabbed my hand with both of his and said: "I'll go to hell if it ain't."

He said he was awfully glad to see me, as he had wondered where I was, and what I was doing. Then he told me that he had prospected over a lot of territory up there, mostly for quartz, and had sold one ledge in Ketchikan that he found and was still getting payments on it. Then he had located two other quartz ledges near there. One was bonded, and the company was running a tunnel on it to see how extensive it was. He was also going to run a tunnel in the other when he got back there. He told me that he had quit drinking, and had got over those crazy spells he used to take, and that I must know that he stood well with the mining people in Alaska or he would not be in charge of the exhibit.

I told him that I did not believe that there was anyone else that was as glad as I was that he had at last found his real self, and I was sure that he had grip enough to hang on to his real self. He asked me to come back in, but I did not have time. I never heard any more from him, but I was happier to see him than anyone else, as it meant a lot to me to know that he was himself again.

I heard that Kingsley Smith and Frank Ahlburg went to the Klondike when they left Cook Inlet, but none of the boys had heard where they were. On one trip to Los Angeles I called up George [A.] Shepard. He and his wife [Jenny] had a cabin near ours in Sunrise, and he worked for Wible the summer I did. The Shepards came out soon after we did and went back to Los Angeles. He said that Mrs. Smith and Addie Alaska were in Los Angeles, but he thought Kingsley and Frank were still somewhere in Alaska.

Some years ago I acquired some property in Phoenix, Arizona, and made trips to look after it. On one trip my son Jim and I stopped overnight in San Francisco with some friends of his. During the evening, some of their friends came in. When they were told that we were on our way to Arizona, one of them said that recently an old Alaska miner had taken him and some friends over there to show them a mine that was for sale.

I asked him what the Alaska miner's name was, and he said "Frank Ahlburg."

"Well," I said, "that's lucky. I know him and had lost track of him."

He told me that Frank was in business in Los Angeles, and was at home most of the time. On my next trip I had an hour between trains and called up Frank. He told me that he had a factory there, and that Kingsley was working for him. He said he had invented a fruit marking machine that was bringing in some income, and that they manufactured a lot of things in the factory.

Frank's good luck followed him all the way, as he married a fine girl. They have had a happy life together and he has been fairly successful. They have one fine daughter. I never saw her, as she was married and living in San Francisco. Of course, Frank has a good head on him, but I know it was luck that saved his neck the day he sailed over the bluff on his snowshoes.

The next trip I stopped off in Los Angeles for a day's visit with him. Kingsley was there for dinner, and of course, we reminisced for hours. They told me of all the places they had been in Alaska, but that they finally gave it up, as neither had struck it rich. They did see a lot of the country, and naturally had a lot of interesting experiences. Frank then came to Los Angeles and got married. He took his wife back to the Klondike with him, and when they got through with Alaska, naturally they came back to Los Angeles. Frank spent the next day with me, showed me over his factory, and then took me over to see my old friend Gus Friberg.

We came back by Addie Alaska Smith's home. Addie Alaska was the first baby born in Sunrise. She had married Byron Geissinger, a nice fellow who was a pharmacist, and they had a nice home and two fine boys. She seemed glad to see me, and said she had heard a lot about me from her parents and

Frank. She asked me a lot of questions about Alaska, said she was writing a history of her parents' experiences up there, and that I could give her some information that she wanted. Of course, I was glad to help her all I could. Her mother was secretary of the club that put on the entertainments at Sunrise, and had kept copies of most of the programs while she was there. It was very interesting to look at them again. Her mother passed away in 1953, and her father in 1955.

U. S. Mercantile Company Store, Sunrise.
ALASKA HISTORICAL COLLECTIONS, ALASKA STATE LIBRARY, JUNEAU.

Addie and Byron liked to travel and made a trip to Alaska as far as Skagway, but never got to her birthplace, old Sunrise. They had arranged to go on a western Canada excursion with a lot of friends from Los Angeles July 10, 1958, but Byron had a heart attack and passed away three days before they expected to leave. She went with the same bunch in 1959, and saw more of the great outdoors up there. No doubt she will find a way to get back to old Sunrise in time. She has her two sons now, and one grandson. That is the little Addie Alaska who played with Mage in our yard the summer of 1899.

I never heard anything more about Mage, but I hope Brownlow buried him there on a nice point if he died over at the lake. It does not matter, though, whether he was buried up there or not, as he has been buried in his old master's heart all these years. And when I pass over the river, if I should wake up on that "Beautiful Isle of Somewhere," I feel sure that Mage will be waiting there to greet me.

INDEX